THE *Spoken* BLESSING I

A Spiritual Posture

Ann Dews Gleaton

First Edition Copyright © 2005 Ann Dews Gleaton

20th Anniversay Edition Copyright © 2025 Ann Dews Gleaton

All rights reserved.

No part of this publication may be reproduced, stored, or transmitted in any form or by any means, including written, copied, or electronically, without prior written permission from the author or her agents. The only exception is brief quotations in printed reviews. Short excerpts may be used with the publisher's or author's expressed written permission.

The Spoken Blessing 1: A Spiritual Posture

Cover design by Carolina Barber Gleaton

ISBN: (Paperback): 9781960024848

ISBN: (e-book): 9781960024855

LCCN:

True Potential, Inc.
PO Box 904, Travelers Rest, SC 29690
www.truepotentialmedia.com

"The Spoken Blessing is a resource I wish I had had when my children were small. I knew words were powerful but never truly realized the full depth of their impact on lives. Ann's book brings the importance of our words and the importance of speaking blessings over our family, friends and others. Speaking blessings can change the whole trajectory of your life. I recommend her book to everyone I encounter who is struggling with relationships. Her personal message along with God's word will bring change in your life."

Pastor Yvonne Dow, All Nations Church, Tallahassee, FL

"Ann Gleaton's *The Spoken Blessing: A Spiritual Posture*, is a timeless treasure and teaching that brings hope to every parent's heart. As Ann so powerfully states in her book, "Those who are blessing others are simply agreeing with God's original desire and plan for 'fruitfulness' and 'multiplication.' Thank you Ann for this wonderful reminder to speak the blessings.*"*

Rebecca Davis Keener, author of Marvelous Motherhood and the Holy Spirit 365 Devotional, Host of Always More TV

"It was indeed an honor to read and greatly benefit from the truths, principles and suggested practices of *The Spoken Blessing*.

What a beautifully written text and one that presents such feeling and application of the Word of God. I was genuinely impacted by the Biblical and personal story lines that validated the intent of the text. It will be my commitment to make more determined, and purpose filled application.

The Apostle Paul in II Corinthians 4:13 declares It is written: 'I believed; therefore I have spoken.' With that same spirit of faith we also declare and believe and therefore speak.

The power and potential of *The Spoken Blessing* is a Biblical privilege and responsibility. I highly encourage you to engage this quality read and allow it to have the authors desired impact upon you and all those you can bless!"

Garry Bryant, Executive Director, Evangelism USA, Author of Jehovah's Blessing

"*The Spoken Blessing* spoke depths into my life. I wish I had this resource when raising my children, yet with family issues now, it gave me a new perspective in praying for my grown children and speaking blessings over their lives. As care pastor of a large church, I see many privileges of praying blessings over those that I care for and those that I love. This book is deep in the Word of God and I can't begin to express how it affected me. I pray that I can put it into practice and perhaps teach others some of the aspects of it. I recommend others to delve into this book and be blessed as I have."

Pastor Sharon Hartman, Salem, Virginia

Acknowledgements

To my loving heavenly Father, my Resurrected Savior, my Holy Comforter: I am forever grateful. You have drawn me to You with love and tenderness, firmness and instruction. Thank You for never leaving nor forsaking me. Thank You for walking and talking with me every day, sharing with me Your precious intimacies and powerful revelations. You are everything to me.

To the man of my dreams, the answer to my prayers, my knight in shining armor: my wonderful husband, Cal, I love you. You are my best friend, the one who touches my heart and soothes my soul. Thank you for walking with me through these years of learning, studying, and teaching, failing and succeeding. Thank you for being there with me.

To our four amazing children: Anthony, Peyton, Elizabeth, and David, their God-ordained spouses: Cassidy, Amy, Kyle and Carolina, and our grandchildren: you are my joy and inspiration for imparting God's blessings. You have brought me so much pleasure in life! You truly are God's gifts to us!

Charlie and Blanche Dews, my parents; Harold and Jeanette Gleaton, Cal's parents: you sowed the good seeds of faith, hope, and trust within us. Thank you for giving us life!

To my sisters, Marti Sappenfield and Libby Markham, and husband, Gary: you have played an important part in my learning how to give and receive God's blessings. Your faithful interest and love have encouraged me to pursue success. Thank you for your loving support.

The Spoken Blessing I: A Spiritual Posture

To Jo Anne Arnett, Laura Mann and Dena Woodburn: thank you for supporting and encouraging me as I pressed on toward the call and directive of God.

To Robert A. Shelley, Kathy Palmer, Dr. Bill Lyons, David and Carol Peleggi of Jerusalem, Israel; and Pastor Bill Ligon of Brunswick, Georgia: you have my deepest appreciation for helping me understand and value our rich Christian heritage as it has been carried forth by the Jewish people—their culture, their language, and their faith in the one, true God.

To our Pastors Steve and Yvonne Dow and friends at All Nations Church in Tallahassee, Florida: thank you for being receptive to the Blessing scrolls and applying them to your lives. We are deeply grateful for your faithful friendships and loving support.

To Ron McCants: I am grateful that you were sensitive and responsive to Holy Spirit's leading. Thank you for introducing me to Steve Spillman and True Media Potential! Cal and I value our friendship with you and Barbara.

To Steve Spillman: Cal and I were encouraged by your sincere interest in creating the 20th Anniversary Edition of this book. Our confidence was boosted as we watched you embrace the vision God has given. The fire in your heart ignited the glowing embers in ours. We needed your support and expertise! Thank you! To God be the Glory! Amen.

Ann Dews Gleaton

Contents

Acknowledgements	5
The Myrtle Tree	9
Foreword	11
Preface	13
Introduction	17
1. Who Began Using the Spoken Blessing?	21
2. What is the Basis for the Spoken Blessing?	45
3. When is the Spoken Blessing Given?	63
4. Where Must We Be Spiritually to Bless Others?	83
5. Why Should We Use the Spoken Blessing?	105
6. Assuming the Spiritual Posture to Bless	125
7. Interning with the Spoken Blessing	147
Appendix	171
Author's Note	177
About the Author:	179
References	181

The Myrtle Tree

"Instead of the thorn shall come up the cypress; instead of the brier shall come up the myrtle; and it shall make a name for the LORD, an everlasting sign that shall not be cut off." (Isaiah 55:13 ESV)

The Myrtle tree is incorporated within the Blessings, etc. logo as a symbol of both God's blessings and His Saints. The Myrtle tree is highly valued and often planted in gardens. It yields choice and excellent fruit for oil and wine. This tree releases a sweet and fragrant scent, never shedding its leaves. The Myrtle tree can be compared to God's people as they are highly esteemed by Him. God plants His spiritual trees, His Saints, within His garden, the Church. They bear fruit to honor Him and to benefit others. Their leaves, which never wither, are for the healing of the nations. God's Saints produce a sweet and pleasing fragrance to Him and others.[1] (Psalm 1:3; Isaiah 60:21; 61:3; Ezekiel 47:12)

What does the myrtle tree mean in Hebrew?

In Hebrew, "myrtle tree" is hadas (הדס) and symbolizes prosperity, restoration, and the beauty that emerges from adversity. The related feminine name is Hadassah (הדסה), meaning "myrtle tree." Queen Esther was known as Hadassah. Her beauty was both natural and spiritual as she humbly served as God's deliverer, restoring His honor among the nations and the freedom of His people.[2]

---

1   Preaching from the Types and Metaphors of the Bible, Benjamin Keach, pp. 761-762
2   https://www.jewishvirtuallibrary.org/myrtle

It is from the heart of God that He restores, exchanging briers for the beauty, fragrance and fruit of the Myrtle Tree. His deep desire is that we prosper in all that we do as we serve Him and others. The longing of God's heart is to fellowship and walk in union with His Saints. He is the Master Gardener of our lives. May our love for Him grow, producing fruit to His glory.

Foreword

What huge anticipation I felt when I heard that Ann Dews Gleaton was in the process of updating and re-printing *The Spoken Blessing*! The principles and examples in this book have such a powerful impact upon the lives of those to whom the blessings are spoken. I have discovered by implementing these principles in my own life that they are very beneficial to those who speak the blessing into other people's lives as well.

Barbara and I met Ann and Cal Gleaton shortly after arriving in Tallahassee, Florida as an associate pastor of the church in which they were leaders. Very quickly, I discovered that spending any amount of time with them was very much an encouragement and a blessing for sure. We were so delighted to get to know them and work very closely together in leadership.

About six months after arriving, she autographed a copy of her book and, of course, gave us a batch of her written blessings in scroll form – a blessing that keeps on giving! The book and the examples of their lives have had a tremendous influence on our lives to this day, almost 20 years later.

As we had read in *The Blessing* by Gary Smalley and John Trent, one of our basic needs is the approval of significant people in our lives, the most vital of which is from our parents. In her book, Ann expands that beyond our family to our faith family and many others who cross our paths in life. It is no coincidence that the first of *The 5 Love Languages* by Gary Chapman is "words of affirmation." Yes, I put *The Spoken Blessing* by Ann Gleaton in the same category as these two classics.

Understanding and seeing the results of employing the spoken blessing will have an incredible impact upon those who put it into practice. There is no one you will ever meet who doesn't need words of encouragement at any given time. "God blesses us so that we might bless others," Dr. Charles Stanley (Life Principle #25). Sometimes we feel as though we do not have a blessing to give because we think of material things, and we may think we have nothing of significance to give. Ann gives us example after example of ways to give through our spoken words that are a lot more valuable than things that are tangible.

She speaks of us as believers being the "living stones" (1 Peter 2:5) and the "light of the world. A city set on a hill..." that Jesus spoke of (Matthew 5:14). Although at times we do not feel as though we are quite spiritual enough or our lives do not measure up to a certain standard to be qualified to bless others, she shows from the word of God that we are conduits of His blessings that He wants to pour out on others.

"By the blessing of the upright a city is exalted, But by the mouth of the wicked it is torn down." (Proverbs 11:11)

As I stated earlier, to be in the presence of Ann and Cal Gleaton is a tremendous encouragement – *The Spoken Blessing* puts you there.

Ron McCants, In Touch Ministries, Pastor, Author, Teacher.

Preface

Sharing Shadows

Muffled weeping came from his room. The figure in the bed was undisturbed by the sounds. His sleep was deep even though his room was full of sorrow. Across the bed, the streetlight cast a shadow of the towering water oak which loomed outside. The weeping came from one who shared her shadow with the oak. The sadness in this mother's heart was as dark as those blended shadows. Another shouting match, harsh, condemning words, and an order to "Go to your room and just go to bed!" had ended this long day.

Thoughts of her son's life—his past, his present, and the predictable future—ran through this mother's mind like a movie. In kindergarten, he had been labeled a "troublemaker," and on numerous occasions, had been sent to stand facing the corner. Upon completion of that year, his attitude was summed up with one statement: "I hate school!" By the time third grade rolled around, his teacher concluded that this dear student was an ADHD (Attention Deficit/Hyperactivity Disorder) child. She wanted him tested and placed on medication to help him pay more attention to his work. This student became angrier by the day. He hated himself because he appeared different from other students. He hated his parents for subjecting him to humiliating psychological testing. He despised walking in the shadow of his older brother and being pestered by his younger sister. Basically, he hated everyone, including God. Walls of resentment and frustration were blocking this child from feeling—feeling anything but anger. Acts of kindness could not penetrate those walls. And that's why his mother was weeping. Hardened hearts and towering walls pointed toward a predictable future: jail time. His mother had lived long enough to have witnessed the relationship of angry hearts, embittered minds, and self-destruction. "No, God, no. Not my son. Don't let it happen to him. I love him so. I hate the way things are. I don't want him to grow up like me."

Her weeping continued, but it was no longer on behalf of her son. She wept over her past—her hardened heart, her bitterness, her unwillingness to forgive. She knew firsthand how destructive those walls around a heart could be to relationships and to one's future. Years and years and many years had been allowed to pass without reconciliation. "Oh, God, things have to change. Help us, God. Help me."

This humbled shadow separated from that of the towering oak as it quietly moved into the darkened house. Weary from crying and weary from worrying, the mother slipped back into her bed. Sleep came, but with a struggle. Life was a struggle, but others weren't to know. She had learned to "grin and bear it," "stuff it and shove it on down." It was no wonder that she suffered from digestive problems. This mother was feeling the effects of the unresolved emotional upheaval that her family was experiencing. Yes, it was affecting the entire family. A major overhaul—that's what was needed.

The Man with a Message

Not long after her night of weeping, this mother heard about a guest speaker who was coming to their church. Pastor Bill Ligon was the son-in-law of a couple within her church. His presentation concentrated on Imparting the Blessing. How that related to her, she wasn't sure, but she insisted that she and her husband attend. At the conclusion of Pastor Ligon's teaching, this mother felt the gratitude and relief of one who had been thrown a life ring as they struggled in a stormy sea. As one being lifted from the overpowering waves, her thoughts screamed through her mind: "Life, not death, is my future. Hope, not despair, can fill my life. Joy, and not sorrow, will overflow from my heart." Things began to change for this mother, for this son, for the whole family as they began to use the principle of the Blessing. Blessings were given and blessings were received, most of the time. Those old walls didn't fall overnight. Rome wasn't built in a day. But those parents did not give up. God had told them to love, love, and keep on loving that son, even when he didn't love back. Hug, hug, and keep on hugging. Bless him in his going out and bless him in his coming in. These parents had to commit to change—change their attitudes, their focus, their hearts.

Dear friends, the family crisis I just described is a "true story." It is our story. The people, the places, the hurts, the painful words and attitudes are real. And so is our God. He was, is, and shall be our Life, our Redeemer and Restorer. He can be yours, as well. The message—the principle of the Spoken Blessing—is His message, His *sent* word for you and yours at this time. The timing is now. Take this message and use it within your family, your friends, your work associates, your fellow believers, and, yes, even strangers. Offer them a cup of cool, refreshing, life-changing water. They will be forever grateful to you and to our God. I know, because I am forever grateful.

Introduction

The Spoken Blessing: A Spiritual Posture

Many individuals are familiar with 'saying the blessing' before eating their meal. Someone speaks a word of thanks to God before the familiar "please pass the green beans" and "I can't wait to taste that homemade bread" begin.

That type of blessing is not the focus of this book.

The focus and foundation of this book is the Spoken Blessing; a term I use to describe a principle I observed occurring within the Bible. From the release of God's creative words which formed His new world, through the verbalized faith of the ancient patriarchs as they trusted God to dwell in the midst of their loved ones, to the impartation of Jesus as he blessed the young children, I recognized a powerful consequence in the spoken release of the word of God. God's original desire was for His image to be multiplied across the face of His world: *"Let Us make man in Our image, according to Our likeness..."* (Genesis 1:26). Verbalized faith is essential to fulfilling God's original instruction to His creations: *"Be fruitful and multiply and fill the earth..."* (Genesis 1:28). God gave mankind the ability to communicate with Him and with others. Faith in God can be multiplied within others as we speak of His mercy and grace. We can verbalize our experience and expectation of His goodness, helping others to recognize and value Him. Valuing God is vital to one's embracing Him. As we speak of His nature, we speak of His image, that is: who He is and what

He does. Communicating this to others is a way of increasing His image across the world.

May the Lord counsel your mind as you carefully read and digest this book.

> *May the eyes of your heart be enlightened*
> *so that you may know*
> *what is the hope of His calling, what are*
> *the riches of the glory of His*
> *inheritance in the saints,*
> *and what is the surpassing greatness*
> *of His power toward you who believe.*
> *In Jesus' Name. Amen.* (Ephesians 1:18-19 NASB)
>
> *A man will be satisfied with good by the fruit of his words, and the deeds of a man's hands will return to him.*
> *The way of a fool is right in his own eyes, But a wise man is he who listens to counsel.* (Proverbs 12:14-15 NASB)

Beloved reader, what posture do you assume before the Lord and before others? Do you listen to *counsel* or are you and your perspective always right? How teachable are you? Will you allow others to correct you? Are you being satisfied *with good*? Can you discern the type of seeds you have sown? What type of harvest are you reaping? Do you need understanding for things that are happening within your life?

"*...those who seek the LORD understand all things.*" (Proverbs 28:5 NASB)

As you seek the Lord, He will help you distinguish between good and evil. He will provide you insight into the situations and events that occur in your life.

"*But if any of you lacks wisdom, let him ask of God, who gives to all men generously and without reproach, and it will be given to him.*"
(James 1:5 NASB)

Asking for help requires humility.

Introduction

Several years ago, I used a hairdresser who was an immigrant. She had "made it on her own." This lady was very proud of her accomplishments and success. God placed us together for a reason. As the months passed, I talked with her about my relationship with the Lord. One day, I inquired if she had ever asked Jesus to be her personal Savior. She quickly snapped back: "No! I've never asked anybody for anything!" We read in Mark 6:1-6 that even Jesus could do only a few miracles within the people of his hometown "due to their unbelief." We should assume a posture of humility *to ask* God for something, to listen to and respond to His reply. We should strive to become a true disciple of Christ, following Him, learning His ways.

If we are a New Testament, New Covenant disciple, then we are not a mere pupil or learner. We adhere to and accept the Lord's instruction that He gives us. We make His instruction our way of living. We become so familiar with the Lord's character and workings that we recognize His hand operating within our lives. To know the Lord, we must spend time with Him. The Lord created us for the pleasure of knowing us, so let's walk and talk with Him, learning His heart's desire, discovering what brings Him joy and excitement. Let us humble ourselves and our desires, to support and assume His goals as our lifetime ambitions.

Consider the disciples who walked and talked with Jesus along the well-known Emmaus Road. Why didn't they recognize Jesus?

"But their eyes were prevented from recognizing Him." (Luke 24:16 NASB)

What prevented these disciples from recognizing Jesus?

"And He said to them, 'O foolish men and slow of heart to believe in all that the prophets have spoken!'" (Luke 24:25 NASB)

Jesus described these disciples as unable to comprehend the precepts and principles of God's Kingdom. He identified the disciples as being slow to embrace and apply His Kingship to the spiritual realm. He understood that they were focusing on their immediate and pressing need for relief from the oppression of Roman rule and dictatorship. Their interpretation and expectation of Jesus' purpose "was right in their own eyes." They had a need, and they expected Him to meet that need according to their way of thinking. They had not humbled themselves to God's purpose for His Messiah. They had been focusing more on their "woes" than on God's "wows."

> *They had been focusing more on their "woes" than on God's "wows."*

The disciples' perception of Jesus affected their ability to recognize or to become well acquainted with Him. Jesus effectively used this situation to God's glory, counseling His disciples and correcting their way of thinking.

The effect that Jesus' Emmaus Road teaching had on those disciples was quite remarkable. Consider their demeanor as Jesus joined them as they walked toward Emmaus.

"And they stood still, looking sad and downcast." (Luke 24:17 AMP)

> *Their "spiritual posture" changed that night.*

Once Jesus had explained the Scriptures to them, once their eyes had been opened to recognize Jesus and their hearts were stirred to believe, their words and actions became excited and uplifted. The disciples were no longer slow or sluggish. They couldn't contain their joy. Their "spiritual posture" changed that night. That very night, they retraced their steps those seven miles and returned to Jerusalem. Their "woes" had been changed to "wows." They had to tell the others. They wanted their new faith in Jesus, their understanding of the Scriptures, to be shared and multiplied within their friends.

And so it is with me. As I share the principle of the Spoken Blessing, may your "woes" be changed to "wows." May the insights into the Scriptures bring new life, energy, and excitement into the very core of your faith in Jesus.

Chapter One
Who Began Using the Spoken Blessing?

So God created the great sea monsters and every living creature that moves, with which the waters swarm, according to their kinds, and every winged bird according to its kind. And God saw that it was good. And God blessed them, saying, "Be fruitful and multiply and fill the waters in the seas, and let birds multiply on the earth."

(Genesis 1:21-22 ESV)

In the beginning, God used the Spoken Blessing to impart the ability to fulfill His plan. God knew the power of His words; the creative force behind them. He desired for His creation, for the Animal Kingdom, to increase in numbers, extending their existence across His newly formed earth.

Then God said, "Let us make man in our image, according to our likeness. And let them have dominion over the fish of the sea and over the birds of the heavens and over the livestock and over all the earth and over every creeping thing that creeps on the earth." So God created man in His own image, in the image of God He created him; male and female He created them. And God blessed them. And God said to them, "Be fruitful and multiply and fill the earth and subdue it, and have dominion over the fish of the sea and over the birds of the heavens and over every living thing that moves on the earth."

(Genesis 1:26-28 ESV)

God's plan was for His image and likeness to be multiplied across the face of the earth. He desired for His character to permeate His created world. Adam and Eve were to serve as His representatives across the earth, having been formed in His image. They had a body, soul, and spirit made in the pattern or likeness of the Holy Trinity.

He blessed them with the ability to fulfill His plan.

God assigned Adam and Eve dominion over His creation. This first couple was given authority and responsibility to cultivate and keep the Garden of Eden. He blessed them with the ability to fulfill His plan.

The service of cultivating or working can be directed toward things, people, or God. Likewise, Adam and Eve were to keep, care for, guard, and preserve the Garden. This is a beautiful and accurate picture of what the Spoken Blessing can do within a person's life. It prepares, breaks up, prevents, preserves, improves, refines, develops, and promotes God's perfect and divine plan for every person.

From the beginning, God has desired for His creation to be blessed and to bless. His instruction was for *blessings* and *increase* to fill, replenish, and cultivate His creation. God knew that sin would challenge the fulfillment of His plan. He knew that Adam and Eve would be forced out of their Paradise and into a harsher world of toil and trouble. God knew that their confidence might suffer defeat. But He had blessed them. And this couple remembered His blessing and impartation of the ability to "be fruitful and multiply."

"Now Adam knew Eve his wife, and she conceived and gave bore Cain, saying, 'I have gotten a man with the help of the LORD.'" (Genesis 4:1 ESV)

Eve recognized the faithfulness of God and His power to fulfill His spoken word. Surely, her confidence increased as she gave birth to her sons, Cain and Abel. Even after the death of Abel, Eve affirmed her faith in God as she gave birth to another son, Seth:

"God has appointed for me another offspring instead of Abel, for Cain killed him." (Genesis 4:25 ESV)

Eve focused her faith and honor toward God, the One who had dominion and power over her life and the future of her family. Her offspring continued to "be fruitful and multiply" as Seth had a son, Enosh. Seth's family chose to honor and trust God:

"...At that time people began to call upon the name of the LORD."
(Genesis 4:26 ESV)

This is the first mention of people praying to God. Men wanted the help of God in their lives. They understood that He was their source. The Scriptures gave prominence to another man who recognized that God was his source.

"These are the generations of Noah. Noah was a righteous man, blameless in his generation. Noah walked with God." (Genesis 6:9 ESV)

Building upon the strength of Noah's relationship with Him, God commanded Noah to construct an ark. God's faithfulness sustained Noah during his prolonged effort amidst a community of evil and berating people.

> *By faith Noah, being warned by God concerning events as yet unseen, in reverent fear constructed an ark for the saving of his household. By this he condemned the world and became an heir of the righteousness that comes by faith.* (Hebrews 11:7 ESV)

Noah was a part of God's plan. The ark was a beautiful foreshadowing of the secret hiding place: the place of refuge that Jesus offers you and me. The ark of Noah saved mankind from total destruction. Jesus saved mankind from total eternal destruction. He is our shelter from the storm. He carries us through troubled waters. He offers us protection from the elements of sin and offers provision for us: body, soul, and spirit.

Now, catch this: *"...Noah, being warned by God concerning events as yet unseen..."* describes our present-day situation. God's word has warned us about events that we have not yet seen, nor can scarcely imagine. Yet, in reverence to our Almighty, All-knowing God, we must help build the ark of Jesus within our family, friends, and others.

> *As he chopped and chiseled, lifted and loaded, Noah spoke of God.*

I suspect that Noah evangelized those who came around during the many years he spent building. The Bible documents that Noah had brothers and sisters (Genesis 5:30). Don't you think that Noah would have tried to share his faith in God with his family members, as well as others in his community? As he chopped and chiseled, lifted and loaded, Noah spoke of God.

God *"did not spare the ancient world, but preserved Noah, a herald of righteousness, with seven others, when he brought a flood upon the world of the ungodly;"* (2 Peter 2:5 ESV)

Remember, Noah walked with God, therefore, Noah *heard* the words of God.

"So then faith cometh by hearing, and hearing by the word of God."
(Romans 10:17 KJV)

As he repeated what God had said, Noah's faith was reinforced and his confidence strengthened. Despite the taunting and mocking, Noah was able to complete God's command.

As we speak a blessing, which is based on the powerful word of God, we exemplify our faith in Him, placing our focus and trust on His steadfast character.

Imagine that you are walking through a large shopping mall and notice someone looking up. You also notice that their focus is fixed. You wonder: "What in the world could be so intriguing?" So, you look up. Then, you see it and gasp at its beauty. Your arm, hand, and finger work instinctively, together, pointing upward. Excitedly, you exclaim, "There it is, I see it. It is beautiful!" Others gather around. The excitement and focus work like a magnet drawing many to peer upward.

That's exactly what will happen when you begin to use the Spoken Blessing. How can I be so sure? My husband, Cal, and I have been speaking blessings over our children for years. The Preface related how our family had hit rock bottom. The only way to look *was* 'up.' We gradually learned how to redirect our focus to the word of God and what He declared about our children, our situations, and our future.

God established the example of blessing children as He blessed Noah and his *sons*, after Noah had prepared an altar and offered burnt offerings to God (Genesis 8:20-9:1-3). We know that God blessed His creation from the beginning and that He wanted His plan to be fulfilled. Within His blessing was His provision. Read Genesis 9:1-3, 7-17 and discover how unceasing God's blessings are. God's covenant and commitment are eternal.

> *This is like the days of Noah to me: as I swore that the waters of Noah should no more go over the earth, so I have sworn that I will not be angry with you, and will not rebuke you.*
>
> *For the mountains may depart and the hills be removed, but my steadfast love shall not depart from you, and my covenant of peace shall not be removed," says the LORD, who has compassion on you.*
>
> *All your children shall be taught by the LORD, and great shall be the peace of your children.* (Isaiah 54:9,10,13 ESV)

Blessings have a long-term effect.

Let's look ahead several generations past Noah, and read about one of his descendants, Abram. The continuous, long-term effect of God's blessings becomes evident as we read His communication with Abram:

> *Now the LORD said to Abram, "Go forth from your country, and from your relatives and from your father's house, to the land which I will show you; and I will make you a great nation, and I will bless you, and make your name great; and so you shall be a blessing; and I will bless those who bless you, and the one who curses you I will curse. And in you all the families of the earth shall be blessed."*
> (Genesis 12:1-3 NASB)

God fully intended for His blessing to flow into and through people.

The Spoken Blessing I: A Spiritual Posture

The Hebrew word used for "bless" is *barak* which means: to kneel down, to bless; praise, to be blessed, pray to, to invoke, to ask a blessing; to greet; to curse; the rendering 'curse' is a Hebrew euphemism.

"Blessing," the English translation of *brakah,* means a blessing, benediction, benefit, favor, peace, invocation of good; a happy, or blessed man.

In studying God's word, I often use Webster's Dictionary to help me understand a word used to define another word, i.e.: *invoke* means "to call on God for a blessing, help; inspiration, protection; to ask solemnly for; implore; entreat."

In these verses, the word *make* is translated from the Hebrew word *asah*: to work, to labor, to create, to construct, to build, to accomplish, to prepare, to keep; to fulfill, to be made; to sacrifice; to appoint. This word describes *God's creative activity*; the *fashioning and refining of His work.*

If God is going to *make* Abram's name *great,* He will be very active in this work. God will be *laboring, creating, building, refining,* and *fashioning* Abram into the man, the husband, the father, the patriarch of a mighty group of people.

When we consider God's original blessing over Adam and Eve, we recall that He intended for there to be *labor* and *cultivation* of that blessing within their lives. In the same way, God committed Himself to such *labor* on behalf of Abram, Sarai and their future family.

Will God do any less for us? We are the future families of which God spoke in His blessing to Abram:

"And in you all the families of the earth shall be blessed."
(Genesis 12:3 NASB)

"Is God the God of Jews only? Is He not the God of Gentiles also? Yes, of Gentiles also, Since indeed God who will justify the circumcised by faith and the uncircumcised through faith is one." (Romans 3:29-30 NASB)

> *For you are all sons of God through faith in Christ Jesus. For all of you who were baptized into Christ have clothed yourselves with Christ. There is neither Jew nor Greek, there is neither slave nor free man, there is neither male nor female; for you are all one in Christ*

Who Began Using the Spoken Blessing?

Jesus. And if you belong to Christ, then you are Abraham's offspring, heirs according to promise. (Galatians 3:26-29 NASB)

God is God to the Jews and the Gentiles. God desires for us to be successful and prosper within His Kingdom; therefore, we can feel confident that He desires to bless us, to labor and work within our lives just as He desired to and executed His plans in the lives of Abram and Sarai.

"For it is God who is at work in you, both to will and to work for His good pleasure." (Philippians 2:13 NASB)

Some may question whether God favors the Jewish people more than the Gentiles. Carefully consider the story in Acts 10. Read this account of Cornelius and the consequences of his reverence toward God, his diligence to seek God through prayer, and his continual effort to honor the Jewish people. Discover the truth that Peter did:

"I most certainly understand now that God is not one to show partiality, but in every nation the man who fears Him and does what is right, is welcome to Him." (Acts 10:34-35 NAS)

In the Middle Eastern culture, males were, and still are, more valued and esteemed than females. Therefore, I found it interesting to discover that Moses, in the writing of Genesis, made a special note of the blessing spoken over Rebekah, the young woman who was to marry Abraham's son, Isaac. Keep in mind that God's original plan and blessing transcended all cultural boundaries which may have restricted a subgroup of people. Turn to Genesis 24 and read Rebekah's blessing. Pay close attention to verse 60: *"And they blessed Rebekah and said to her: May you, our sister, become thousands of ten thousands, and may your descendants possess the gate of those who hate them."*

The phrase "thousands of ten thousands" is used figuratively to represent the extreme---an indefinite number or one that is innumerable. Rebekah's family expected great increase, dominion and authority to flow into and through her life.

Consider this: Rebekah did become the mother of thousands---truly, millions. By the time Moses led the children of Israel out of Egypt, their numbers had grown to millions. Review God's blessing that He spoke over Abram in (Genesis 12:1-3).

"And I will make you a great nation, and I will bless you, and make your name great." (Genesis 12:2 NASB)

Through God's perfect design and plan, He coupled these two blessings to complement each other.

Abram's son, Isaac, carried that blessing into his marriage with Rebekah. Through God's perfect design and plan, He coupled these two blessings to complement each other. Webster's helps us here: *complement* is *that which completes or brings to perfection.*

Let's make a Life Application at this point.

Life Application:

Cal and I have spoken blessings over our children since their youth. Within those blessings, we have released, by faith, God's provision for their spouses and children. Those blessings were accompanied by continuous prayers. We trusted the Father's heart to accomplish His will and good pleasure within their present and future lives. Cal and I expressed our confidence in God to direct our children to the one He had prepared for them, just as He directed Abraham's servant across hundreds of miles to locate Abraham's relatives. We can testify that across the distance of time and space, God brought forth spouses who carry a blessing complementing---*bringing into perfection*---those blessings we have spoken over our children. Truly we stand in awe of God.

I recognize that a person may remain single and feel completed through their relationship with the Lord (Matthew 19:10-12). I do not deny that. Yet, Cal and I can personally testify to God's complementing our individual gifting and calling through each other. I may not be adept or proficient in something, but Cal is, and vice versa. We appreciate each other's abilities and assist the other when needed. Unity---oneness in body, soul and spirit---is our goal, as is God's goal. He has declared us as *one, therefore,* we equally share in the honor of serving Him and share in the responsibility and authority of serving others. We are co-laborers in God's Kingdom. *"And the two shall become one."* (Matthew 19:5-6; Genesis 2:24)

Speaking blessings is used to impart the ability to fulfill God's plan. We must, continually, direct our faith, focus and speech to God's ultimate, eternal purposes.

"Thy kingdom come, Thy will be done, in earth as it is in heaven."
(Matthew 6:10 KJV)

Within the well-known Lord's Prayer, Jesus was instructing His disciples on the importance of their submission and commitment to God's ultimate plans and purposes for His kingdom. We must keep our eyes focused on Jesus' directive to advance God's Kingdom across the earth.

Return with me to the intriguing saga of Isaac and Rebekah. Read Genesis 26:1-5. Look at God's blessing that was spoken over Isaac. Does it not repeat and confirm His blessing for Abraham?

> *Now Isaac sowed in that land, and reaped in the same year a hundredfold. And the LORD blessed him, and the man became rich, and continued to grow richer until he became very wealthy; for he had possessions of flocks and herds and a great household, so that the Philistines envied him.* (Genesis 26:12-14 NASB)

After Isaac experienced repeated conflict with his neighbors, he found a place of rest and called the well *Rehoboth,* which meant *plenty of room.* He confessed his faith in God's provision and commitment to His blessing as noted in Genesis 26:22 NASB: *"At last the LORD has made room for us, and we shall be fruitful in the land."*

Then God appeared to Isaac, reassuring him of His eternal destiny for him: *"I am the God of your father Abraham; do not fear, for I am with you. I will bless you, and multiply your descendants, for the sake of My servant Abraham."* (Genesis 26:24 NASB)

Isaac had personally experienced the spoken blessing of God and the fulfillment of His word. God set forth the example of speaking blessings over others; therefore, it should not surprise us to observe Isaac's deep desire to bless his son, Esau, his firstborn. Turn to Genesis 27:1-4:

"...that my soul may bless you before I die." (NASB)

The Hebrew understanding of *soul* was the *inner self*. Thus, Isaac indicated that his deepest desire was to bless his son with everything that was within him. Isaac carried within his total inner being the blessing that God had commanded over his father, Abraham, as well as over himself.

The Source of our blessing is God.

Much has been written about Rebekah and Jacob's deception of Isaac, which resulted in the younger brother, Jacob, receiving Esau's firstborn blessing. Throughout generations, the Bible documented that great value was placed on the blessing of the firstborn son, for it confirmed his birthright, which carried pre-eminence, authority and provision. God had spoken to Rebekah when she was still carrying her twins. He explained His plans for her boys:

"Two nations are in your womb; and two peoples shall be separated from your body; and one people shall be stronger than the other; and the older shall serve the younger." (Genesis 25:23 NASB)

She stepped in to "help God out."

Before her boys were born, Rebekah knew that the younger, Jacob, would ultimately rule over his older brother, Esau. So, when she overheard Isaac instructing Esau to prepare a meal for his blessing, she stepped in to *help God out*. She didn't trust God to accomplish what He said He would do. This is a lesson for us! Just where is our trust level? Is there anything too hard for the Lord? (Genesis 18:14) Our words will quickly say, "No!" Yet, what do our actions say?

Beloved of God, be careful not to take matters into your own hands. Deception and defiance are insidious. Parents and children can make mistakes, that includes us. We suffer the consequences of our actions. Those mistakes are painful for God and for us.

The Bible is full of examples of both---children and parents suffering the results of their choices. Rebekah truly suffered because of her deception and rebellion. It cost her the pleasure of her favorite son's companionship. Rebekah continued her deception as she persuaded Isaac to send

Who Began Using the Spoken Blessing?

Jacob away: *"I am tired of living, because of the daughters of Heth; if Jacob takes a wife from the daughters of Heth, like these, from the daughters of the land, what good will my life be to me?"* (Genesis 27:46 NASB)

A question that every believer must answer is: "Do I trust God with the future?"

Picture this: you are in a thick crowd of people who are gradually shifting closer to the edge of the street. The police are controlling your advance, holding everyone at the curb. As the crowd, filled with anticipation, pushes closer together to see the approaching excitement, you notice a tall man hoisting a young child up to his shoulders. This pair looks expectantly as the man points in the direction of the advancing parade.

Let's apply this scenario to that of a parent who speaks blessings over their children. Every parent should deeply desire that their children succeed and prosper to a higher level or degree than they have. As devoted parents, we should *lift* our children onto our shoulders, helping them *see* and experience their future destiny that is *down the road* and soon to arrive. Releasing blessings into their lives can assist them in that effort.

> *Those who are blessing others are simply agreeing with God's original desire and plan for "fruitfulness" and "multiplication."*

The Spoken Blessing places an expectation upon Almighty God to exercise His power, authority and blessing over people. Those who are blessing others are simply agreeing with God's original desire and plan for "fruitfulness" and "multiplication."

Why was Rebekah so forlorn? Could it be that she recognized her failure to undergird her sons in attaining their God-appointed destinies? Painfully, she could have realized that she had worked *against* that fulfillment, attempting to *help God out*. Her manipulation cost her dearly.

Beloved of God, please take this lesson to heart. Learn from it. Now, is anything too hard for the Lord? Absolutely not! His mercies are new every morning. His grace is sufficient for us! Thank you, Lord, thank you.

The Spoken Blessing I: A Spiritual Posture

Did or will God ignore His covenant relationship with His people? Absolutely not! God responded to Isaac's blessing that he spoke over Jacob (Genesis 27:27-29). As Jacob lived out his life under that blessing, he followed his father's example by prophesying over and blessing his sons. Grandparents, notice that in chapter 48 of Genesis, Jacob blessed his grandsons, Joseph's sons, Ephraim and Manasseh. Our grandchildren treasure our blessings!

"Then Jacob summoned his sons and said, 'Assemble yourselves that I may tell you what shall befall you in the days to come.'" (Genesis 49:1 NASB)

The Hebrew word for *"tell"* is *Nagad*, "to front, that is, stand boldly out opposite; to manifest; figuratively to announce (always by word of mouth to one present); specifically to expose, predict, explain, praise, certify, declare (-ing), denounce, expound, messenger, profess, rehearse, report, shew (forth), speak, tell, utter." (Strong's Concordance)

Read the next verse: *"Gather together and hear, O sons of Jacob; and listen to Israel your father."* (Genesis 49:2 NASB) *Hear* and *listen* are the same Hebrew word: *shama*-- to hear intelligently (often with implication of attention, obedience): attentively, consent, consider, discern, give ear, listen, obey, perceive, (make a) proclaim (-ation), publish, regard, report, shew (forth), tell, understand, witness." (Strong's Concordance)

As you read Jacob's blessings for each son (Genesis 49:3-27), pay close attention to the *curses* which were spoken because of the behaviors of some of Jacob's sons: Reuben, Simeon, and Levi. Consider Jacob's firstborn, Reuben:

Reuben, you are my firstborn, my might, and the firstfruits of my strength, preeminent in dignity and preeminent in power. Unstable as water, you shall not have preeminence, because you went up to your father's bed; then you defiled it---he went up to my couch! (Genesis 49:3,4 ESV)

Continue reading Jacob's prophecy regarding the next two sons:

Simeon and Levi are brothers; weapons of violence are their swords. Let my soul come not into their council; O my glory, be not joined to their company. For in their anger they killed men, and in their willfulness they hamstrung oxen. Cursed be their anger, for it is fierce, and their wrath, for it is cruel! I will divide them in Jacob and scatter them in Israel. (Genesis 49:5,6,7 ESV)

"The character of each was delineated with unerring insight: the outstanding incidents of their past history enumerated and their future forecasted." (e-Sword X)

The word *cursed* is the Hebrew word *arar*. It means "to bind (with a spell); to hem in with obstacles; to render powerless to resist." (*Lexicon to the Old and New Testaments,* Spiros Zodhiates, Th.D.)

Strong's Concordance adds more insight to the depth of Jacob's disapproval and disdain for his sons' actions: "to execrate; bitterly curse." To *execrate* means to *"feel or express great loathing for."* (*Oxford Languages*)

In essence, Jacob rendered discipline for the actions of his two sons, Simeon and Levi, by *hemming in their anger and wrath, curtailing or restraining their behavior.*

> Jacob's curse on Simeon and Levi (vv. 5-7) would happen only if they kept on making unwise choices. All the curses and all the blessings mentioned in this chapter [Genesis 49] depended on the sons' choices. This is called "conditional" blessings or curses. For example, centuries later, because of how the Levites (i.e., the family of Levi) stood as holy representatives for God while others worshiped an idol (the golden calf), the curse was removed and replaced by a blessing and a position of honor (Ex. 32:26-29; Lev. 25:32-33; Deut. 10:8; 33:8-11). Curses that a family suffers because of a father's (or mother's) poor choices can be broken and removed if children down the family line repent and turn to God (Lev. 26:39-42; 2 Chr. 30:7-9; Jer. 31:29-30; Ezek. 18:1-9). {FireBible, p. 83, note on Genesis 49:7 ESV, brackets added}

The birthright of the firstborn, Reuben, was taken from him because he defiled his father's bed. Reuben's succumbing to his sexual lusts stripped him and his descendants of authority and dominion. He honored his physical lusts more than his birthright, more than his eternal destiny.

"A lack of character that results in moral failure can remove or permanently prevent a person from holding a position of spiritual leadership." (FireBible, p. 83, note on Genesis 49:4 ESV)

The Spoken Blessing I: A Spiritual Posture

1 Chronicles 5:1 identifies the recipient of Reuben's birthright:

> *The sons of Reuben the firstborn of Israel (for he was the firstborn, but because he defiled his father's couch, his birthright was given to the sons of Joseph the son of Israel, so that he could not be enrolled as the oldest son; though Judah became strong among his brothers and a chief came from him, yet the birthright belonged to Joseph.*

Reading 1 Chronicles 5:2 (ASV) we discover: *"For Judah prevailed above his brethren, and of him came the prince; but the birthright was Joseph's."*

Jesus, our Prince of Peace, came through Judah's line.

Turn to Genesis 49:8-12 and read Judah's blessing. Jacob prophesied about Jesus (Rev. 5:5).

Choices and actions result in consequences. This is also seen in the New Testament:

> *Do not be deceived. God is not mocked; for whatever a man sows, this he will also reap. For the one who sows to his own flesh shall from the flesh reap corruption, but the one who sows to the Spirit shall from the Spirit reap eternal life.* (Galatians 6:7-8 NASB)

"For the Son of Man is going to come in the glory of His Father with His angels; and will then recompense every man according to his deeds."
(Matthew 16:27 NASB)

Webster's explains *recompense*: to "repay (a person, etc.); reward; compensate. (n): something given or done in return for something else; repayment; remuneration; something given or done to make up for a loss, injury, etc."

> *Each man's work will become evident; for the day will show it, because it is to be revealed with fire; and the fire itself will test the quality of each man's work. If any man's work which he has built upon it remains, he shall receive a reward.* (I Corinthians 3:13-14 NASB)

Read Genesis 49:28 (NASB): *"All these are the twelve tribes of Israel, and this is what their father said to them when he blessed them. He blessed them, every one with the blessing appropriate to him."*

We can glean *truths* from this statement. Jacob was inspired by God's Holy Spirit as he foretold or prophesied the events which would occur within each son's lineage. Jacob's sons received whatever was suitable to him. We, too, can be led by the Spirit to speak blessings.

Life Application:

When we bless our children, grandchildren and others, we move into the authority of speaking encouragement for Christ-like actions and discipline for selfish choices. We know God's will because we have become students of God's inerrant word and we know the character of Christ.

Recently, three of our grandsons graduated from elementary and middle school. As Cal and I prepared blessings to speak and declare over them, we included blessings that paved a path of behavior and choices that reflected the character of Jesus. Both of us recognized the need to direct their focus and path. We would speak God's word *over* and *before* them since *"Thy word is a lamp unto my feet, and a light unto my path."*
(Psalm 119:105 KJV)

Please read verse 105 in The Passion Translation: *"Truth's shining light guides me in my choices and decisions; the revelation of your word makes my pathway clear."*

Isn't that what we want for our children, grandchildren, ourselves and others? We deeply desire that the revealed word of God clarifies and directs daily decisions.

The Passion Translation provides this rendering for James 1:18: *"God was delighted to give us birth by the truth of his infallible Word so that we would fulfill his chosen destiny for us and become the favorite ones out of all his creation!"*

We gain a deeper understanding of God's will as we study His word and draw close to Him. To stand in the spiritual authority or *posture* to effectively speak a blessing, we must be a student and a doer of God's word (James 1:22). Knowing God, the Father, and His Son, the Word, and being directed and inspired by Holy Spirit, we can *tell, announce, proclaim,* even *celebrate with praise,* the things that are to come within the lives of others.

> *This is the key to releasing the Spoken Blessing within the lives of others: developing and maintaining deep intimacy with God through His Spirit who lives within us.*

Jacob knew what blessing was *appropriate* for each son because he was led by God's Spirit as he prophesied. I found it interesting to compare the *action verb* used in Genesis 49:1, *to tell* [to declare, to make known, to reveal something which one would not otherwise know, to celebrate with praise] and the *action verb* used in verse 28 of that chapter: *to bless,* [to praise, to invoke, to ask a blessing].

If we are *celebrating* something, we assume a certain mental and emotional posture of success, victory, authority, and knowledge. Likewise, we assume a similar spiritual posture as we declare, announce, *celebrate* and bless others with God's word through releasing *the Spoken Blessing.*

As we live under the New Covenant and not the Old, we have an advantage over the Old Testament people in several ways:

1. We have the fuller scope of God's revealed will for our instruction and training:

Every Scripture is God-breathed (given by His inspiration) and profitable for instruction, for reproof and conviction of sin, for correction of error and discipline in obedience, [and] for training in righteousness (in holy living, in conformity to God's will in thought, purpose, and action), so that the man of God may be complete and proficient, well fitted and thoroughly equipped for every good work. (II Timothy 3:16-17 AMP)

> *Releasing the Spoken Blessing into the lives, into the future of others, is a "good work."*

2. Living within us, we have God's Holy Spirit who shares God's revelation:

But the Comforter (Counselor, Helper, Intercessor, Advocate, Strengthener, Standby), the Holy Spirit, Whom the Father will send in My name [in My place, to represent Me and act on My behalf], He will teach you all things. And He will cause you to recall (will remind you of, bring to your remembrance) everything I have told you. (John 14:26 AMP)

Now may our Lord Jesus Christ himself, and God our Father, who loved us and gave us eternal comfort and good hope through grace, comfort your hearts and establish them in every good work and word.
(2 Thessalonians 2:16-17 ESV)

"Encourage your hearts and inspire you with strength to always do and speak what is good and beautiful in his eyes."
(2 Thessalonians 2:17 TPT)

3. We have access to God's throne through our Lord Jesus, our Mediator:

"But now He has obtained a more excellent ministry, by as much as He is also the mediator of a better covenant, which has been enacted on better promises." (Hebrews 8:6 NASB)

"For Christ did not enter a holy place made with hands, a mere copy of the true one, but into heaven itself, now to appear in the presence of God for us." (Hebrews 9:24 NASB)

For the Messiah did not enter into the earthly tabernacle made by men, which was but an echo of the true sanctuary, but he entered into heaven itself to appear before the face of God in our place.
(Hebrews 9:24 TPT)

Since therefore, brethren, we have confidence to enter the holy place by the blood of Jesus, let us draw near with a sincere heart in full assurance of faith, having our hearts sprinkled clean from an evil conscience and our bodies washed with pure water. Let us hold fast the confession of our hope without wavering, for He who promised is faithful; and let us consider how to stimulate one another to love and good deeds. (Hebrews 10:19, 22-24 NASB)

Stimulate, according to Webster's Dictionary, means *"to rouse to action or increased action, as by goading; spur on; excite."*

In Jacob's parting words, he deeply desired *to rouse to action,* to urge his sons on toward their destiny with God. When we speak a blessing into someone's life, we are *stimulating them* to pursue their fullest potential in God's Kingdom. The focus of our blessings should be to love God, to love others, and to do good deeds for His Kingdom.

> *And now we are brothers and sisters in God's family because of the blood of Jesus, and he welcomes us to come right into the most holy sanctuary in the heavenly realm—boldly and with no hesitation. Discover creative ways to encourage others and to motivate them toward acts of compassion, doing beautiful works as expressions of love.* (Hebrews 10:19,24 TPT)

Even as Egyptian slaves, Jacob's sons became a great nation. God desired for His blessing and presence to be continually experienced by these people. Moses and Aaron were instructed by God:

> *Thus you shall bless the sons of Israel. You shall say to them: 'The LORD bless you, and keep you; the LORD make His face shine on you, and be gracious to you; the LORD lift up His countenance on you, and give you peace.' So they shall invoke My name on the sons of Israel, and I then will bless them.* (Numbers 6:23-27 NASB)

Life Application:

It is very important to bless others "in the name of the Lord," because you are engaging the name that is above every name, the name of our Creator, the One who died for us; you are asking for His divine image to be infused into each situation. His name reflects His image. God's creation plan was for His image to be multiplied across the face of the earth.

When I speak or write a blessing to someone, I end it with: "In Jesus' Name." Jesus was very clear in His instruction to us:

> *"And whatever you ask in My name, that will I do, that the Father may be glorified in the Son. If you ask Me anything in My name, I will do it."*
> (John 14:13-14 NASB)

Who Began Using the Spoken Blessing?

> *We bless others in a manner that God would choose to bless.*

Now, I realize that *blessing* and *asking* are two different verbs, two actions. Yet, at work here is the same principle of invoking the total character and nature of our God to operate within a person's life. When we unite our spirit with His Spirit, when we make His desire, our desire, then, whatever we ask *will* line up with or agree with His nature and character. That is why it is so important to know God intimately. We bless others in a manner that God would choose to bless.

Let's review for a moment. We have seen how God set the example of speaking life and blessings over His creation. He continued to impart the ability to fulfill His plan as He blessed Noah, Abram, and Isaac. We read the beautiful and powerful blessing that Isaac called forth over Jacob. Continuing the heritage of *the Spoken Blessing*, Jacob blessed his sons. As the fulfillment of God's plan continued, Jesus followed His Father's example and explained His ways:

> *Truly, truly I say to you, the Son can do nothing of Himself, unless it is something He sees the Father doing; for whatever the Father does, these things the Son also does in like manner: For the Father loves the Son, and shows Him all things that He Himself is doing; and greater works than these will He show Him, that you may marvel. For just as the Father raises the dead and gives them life, even so the Son also gives life to whom He wishes.* (John 5:19-21 NASB)

Turn to Mark 10:13-16 to read about some very determined parents. Are we as determined to get our children to Jesus? Do we possess and exercise the *faith*, *commitment*, and *expectation* these parents had as they refused to be denied the opportunity for their children to be blessed by Jesus? Look at what they did! Jesus' disciples tried to block their divine appointment with Jesus because they didn't perceive the children as being worthy of Jesus' time and audience. Honestly, we should learn several things here:

1. Jesus considers the lowliest of people to be worthy of His love and attention.

2. Jesus is always setting forth an example of an attitude and behavior that we are to follow *in like manner.*

3. Jesus desires to bless and motivate every person to attain their destiny within God's Kingdom.

4. As believers, we are to exhibit our *faith* in Jesus, *commitment* to His goals, and *expectation* of His power and authority operating within our lives.

5. As spiritual people, we should remain humble and submissive to correction and redirection from our Lord. We must always remember that His ways are higher than our ways; His thoughts are higher than our thoughts (Isaiah 55:9).

Jesus released His *faith, commitment,* and *expectation* within us, as His disciples, when He said:

Truly, truly I say to you, he who believes in Me, the works that I do shall he do also; and greater works than these shall he do; because I go to the Father. And whatever you ask in My name, that will I do, that the Father may be glorified in the Son. If you ask Me anything in My name, I will do it. (John 14:12-14 NASB)

He wants us to call upon Him, to do *greater* works than He did. I don't declare that in an arrogant way. I emphasize His intentions for us to walk in and with His authority, dominion, and power. We must know His character. When we do, we can speak, with confidence, His blessings upon people. And how do we know His character? We must devour His life-depositing word; we must internalize it; we must abide with Him, allowing His character to overtake our own. He must increase as we decrease (John 3:30).

In the beginning was the Word, and the Word was with God, and the Word was God. He was in the beginning with God. And the Word became flesh, and dwelt among us, and we beheld His glory, glory as of the only begotten from the Father, full of grace and truth.
(John 1:1,2,14 NASB)

We are to speak God's word as we release *the Spoken Blessing* into people's lives. As His Spirit lives within us, the Spirit will bring to our remembrance the words of Christ that are appropriate for every situation and need. Even when we don't understand how the *remembered* scripture relates to the person, we are to trust in His Spirit's direction, speaking with confidence. We will discover that the blessing we speak will be *right on time* and *just the right fit* for that person.

Who used *the Spoken Blessing*? God did.

Who should use *the Spoken Blessing*? We should, allowing God's Spirit to speak through us.

Declare with me:

God, I recognize You as the source of all my blessings.

I humble myself before You and others to receive blessings.

I turn my heart, mind, and soul towards heaven, ready to hear Your blessings for others.

Teach me to know Your voice and to heed Your instruction.

I want to follow Your example of blessing others.

Counsel my heart that I might know Your will.

In Jesus' Name, Amen.

Journal of My Journey with the Spoken Blessing

God used *the Spoken Blessing* to ...
_____
_____
_____

I will use blessings to ...
_____
_____
_____

As I speak blessings over others, I expect ...
_____
_____
_____

I will ask Holy Spirit to show me ...
_____
_____
_____

I will follow the example of Jesus when He ...
_____
_____
_____

Who Began Using the Spoken Blessing?

Write a blessing to help someone's heart change from 'bitter' to "better."

_____
_____
_____
_____

"A joyful heart makes a cheerful face, but when the heart is sad, the spirit is broken." (Proverbs 15:13 NASB)

Chapter Two

What is the Basis for the Spoken Blessing?

The Spoken Blessing is founded upon God's:

1. commitment to His creation
2. commitment to His covenant
3. commitment to His name, His nature, His image.

> *Then God spoke to Noah and to his sons with him, saying, 'Now behold, I Myself do establish My covenant with you, and with your descendants after you; and with every living creature that is with you—the birds, the cattle, and every beast of the earth with you—of all that comes out of the ark, even every beast of the earth.... And I will establish My covenant with you; and all flesh shall never again be cut off by the water of the flood, neither shall there again be a flood to destroy the earth.' and I will remember My covenant, which is between Me and you and every living creature of all flesh; and never again shall the water become a flood to destroy all flesh.*
> (Genesis 9:8-11,15 NASB)

God showed a commitment to His creation by blessing them. We reviewed this in the first chapter (Genesis 1:21-22, 26-31). He called upon Himself, the fullness of the Godhead---God, the Father; God, the Son; God, the Holy Spirit---to assist and empower His creation to fulfill the original mandate.

The Spoken Blessing I: A Spiritual Posture

In God's instruction to His people, He commanded certain ways of dealing with others and with Himself. Keep in mind that whatever God expected of His people, He would perform no less. If He recognized that *taking an oath* or *making a vow* created a binding obligation (Numbers 30:1-2), then He would place the same or stricter requirement upon Himself. We were created in His image.

> *When you make a vow to the LORD your God, you shall not delay to pay it, for it would be sin in you, and the LORD your God will surely require it of you.... You shall be careful to perform what goes out from your lips, just as you have voluntarily vowed to the LORD your God, what you have promised.* (Deuteronomy 23:21,23 NASB)

In earlier times, when a person made a vow---a solemn promise or pledge---to the Lord, they were to be prompt in paying it. Likewise, the Lord placed the same requirements of promptness and commitment upon Himself. His people were admonished to perform what goes out from their lips. He did, also. Male and female were created in His image. Therefore, if God wanted mankind to act in this or that way, He would do the same, because He was the original Being from which the images were made.

Read Genesis 9:6, which states that anyone who sheds the blood of another, will have his own blood shed because that act attacks the image of God.

Even when God felt it necessary to purge the earth and judge mankind for their flagrant sinfulness, He preserved man, His creatures, and His world, continuing His commitment to His creation. After the Flood, God was quick to reaffirm His covenant with Noah and his sons:

> *And God blessed Noah and his sons and said to them, "Be fruitful and multiply, and fill the earth. And as for you, be fruitful and multiply; populate the earth abundantly and multiply in it."*
> (Genesis 9:1,7 NASB)

> *And God said, "This is the sign of the covenant which I am making between Me and you and every living creature that is with you, for all successive generations: I set My bow in the cloud, and it shall be for a sign of a covenant between Me and the earth. And it shall come*

What is the Basis for the Spoken Blessing?

> *about, when I bring a cloud over the earth, that the bow shall be seen in the cloud, and I will remember My covenant, which is between Me and you and every living creature of all flesh; and never again shall the water become a flood to destroy all flesh."*
> (Genesis 9:12-15 NASB)

God established an eternal covenant with mankind and with every living creature. He confirmed a covenant that He would always remember *"for all successive generations."* Following Noah's *"successive generations,"* we discover that the Lord instructed a man to 'think outside the box,' to 'color outside the lines.' God challenged this man to go beyond what he could see or imagine.

God called this man to trust Him.

> *Now the Lord said to Abram, "Go forth from your country, and from your relatives and from your father's house, to the land which I will show you; and I will make you a great nation, and I will bless you, and make your name great; and so you shall be a blessing;* [Blessing---Brakah: benefit, favor, peace, a gift or present to gain goodwill] *and I will bless those who bless you, and the one who curses you I will curse. And in you all the families of the earth shall be blessed."*
> (Genesis 12:1-3 NASB, brackets added)

Doesn't that last phrase. *"and in you all the families of the earth shall be blessed,"* reflect God's covenant promise with Noah: *"for all successive generations?"* Abram was a recipient of Noah's blessing from God, but it didn't stop with him. God declared it and He caused it to happen. Blessings flowed through Abram onto others. God established the pattern for releasing *the Spoken Blessing*: an ever-continuing ripple effect.

In Genesis 17:1-9, God carefully identified the covenant responsibilities of both parties: Himself and Abram. Take note of God's part and Abram's part, and the longevity of both.

> *Now when Abram was ninety-nine years old, the LORD appeared to Abram and said to him, "I am God Almighty; walk before Me, and be blameless. And I will establish My covenant between Me and you, and I will multiply you exceedingly." And Abram fell on his face, and God talked with him, saying, "As for Me, behold, My covenant*

> *is with you, and you shall be the father of a multitude of nations. No longer shall your name be called Abram, but your name shall be Abraham; for I will make you the father of a multitude of nations. And I will make you exceedingly fruitful, and I will make nations of you, and kings shall come forth from you. And I will establish My covenant between Me and you and your descendants after you throughout their generations for an everlasting covenant, to be God to you and to your descendants after you. And I will give to you and to your descendants after you, the land of your sojournings, all the land of Canaan, for an everlasting possession; and I will be their God.' God said further to Abraham, 'Now as for you, you shall keep My covenant, you and your descendants after you throughout their generations."* (Genesis 17:1-9 NASB)

God Almighty's commitment to His covenant continued to be upheld throughout the generations. And in *"the fullness of the time,"* God's promised Messiah, Savior, and Redeemer, was brought into the world.

> *But when the fullness of the time came, God sent forth His Son, born of a woman, born under the Law, in order that He might redeem those who were under the Law, that we might receive the adoption as sons. And because you are sons, God has sent forth the Spirit of His Son into our hearts, crying, "Abba! Father!" Therefore you are no longer a slave, but a son; and if a son, then an heir through God."*
> (Galatians 4:4-7 NASB)

Jesus brought with Him a new and better covenant through the shedding of His blood on Calvary.

II Corinthians 3:4-6 (NASB) describes our new covenant:

> *And such confidence we have through Christ toward God. Not that we are adequate in ourselves to consider anything as coming from ourselves, but our adequacy is from God, who also made us adequate as servants of a new covenant, not of the letter, but of the Spirit; for the letter kills, but the Spirit gives life.*

This is a true and accurate description of the ministry of the Spirit as we speak blessings upon others. We are not adequate; we are not sufficient to accomplish this work by ourselves. Our adequacy is from God. His grace is sufficient for us, enabling us to achieve God's will and His good pleasure. We desire to release into others' lives: life, hope, love for the Lord, and a fulfillment of their destiny. We are servants of the new and better covenant, executing our King's decree. Just as messengers personally carried the King's word, near and far, to his subjects, we carry forth our King's message which is expressed through His declared word.

As you begin a life of speaking blessings over people, they will associate you with one who brings glad tidings which encourage, uplift, and transform their lives.

Through the power and presence of His Spirit living within us, empowering us to release His word, we can *speak life*, not death, into our fellow servants. As you begin a life of speaking blessings over people, they will associate you with one who brings *glad tidings*, which encourage, uplift, and transform their lives. They will receive your blessings as one who has run a long, hot race and needs a bucket of cool, refreshing water poured over them. That hot and weary soul is noticeably revived by the water flowing over them. I have watched runners tilt their heads and mouths upward, attempting to drink some of the water. A recovery occurs within that runner. A restoration begins. A body is renewed.

Keep this visual image in your mind as you set out to carry your King's message as you begin to speak blessings over people. You will experience this very thing! It is so thrilling to be the pourer of that life-giving water! Speaking blessings will become a delight to you and to your Lord.

May I highlight something here:

For many years, I lived my life as a believer without grasping the truth, nor experiencing the reality of God's Spirit living within me. From the moment I accepted Jesus as my Savior, He took up residency, yet, I didn't understand this aspect of my Christian life. Over the years, I recognized a deep yearning within me which needed to be satisfied. As I searched for fulfillment, I discovered God's treasure: Holy Spirit residing within me. Wanting to know Jesus in a deeper, more powerful way, I submitted more and more of *myself* to the teaching and leading of His Spirit. Then,

I experienced His perfecting the nature and character of the Lord Jesus within me. When we accept the gift of salvation from Jesus, we have the promise of His Holy Spirit living within us (John 14:16,17,26; Acts 1:8; I Corinthians 12:12-13).

Consider the following analogy of the presence of God's Holy Spirit residing within our lives:

I receive a notice that a wealthy relative has bequeathed to me his beautiful home. I have a choice to accept or decline this gift. I choose to accept. As I am handed the keys to this elaborate house, the officiator of the will explains something: there is a permanent resident, a respected guest, who lives in the house. He will offer his help and friendship as often or as much as I permit. The choice of developing the friendship is mine. As I *test the waters* of this friendship, I discover the joy of getting to know this guest. As I encounter the challenges of life, I go to him for help and counsel. Interestingly, he is always willing to assist me. His wisdom is far greater than mine. Our friendship develops into one in which I am eager to spend time with him every day. I need our times together. His advice—his words—encourage and strengthen me, preparing me for the responsibilities of every day. I invite him to accompany me throughout my day. He's such a comfort to me. We walk and talk together. I share my heart with him. He shares his with me. There comes a time in my life in which my desires begin reflecting his. Seeing the future through his eyes becomes an important goal for me. I want what he wants.

As we give God's Spirit more room to operate within our submitted lives, the greater influence and effect He has within us. Our life matures to the point where we can offer encouragement, truth, and peace to others. The Kingdom of God is present within a life that is submitted to God. Our life is focused on expanding and encouraging the preeminence of His Kingdom within the hearts and lives of others.

II Corinthians 4:6,7 (NASB) explains God's promised treasure, His Spirit:

> *For God, who said, 'Light shall shine out of darkness,' is the One who has shone in our hearts to give the light of the knowledge of the glory of God in the face of Christ. But we have this treasure in earthen vessels, that the surpassing greatness of the power may be of God and not from ourselves.*

God desires His people to be clothed and filled with His powerful nature as they had experienced in the Garden.

"And the man and his wife were both naked and were not ashamed."
(Genesis 2:25 NASB)

They were innocent, pure, safe and secure. They listened only to God's voice and trusted in His provision for them. Adam and Eve enjoyed walking and talking with their Creator.

Then sin tempted their hearts and caused them to doubt the character of God and the authority of His word. Their innocent trust in God was shattered. They lost their sense of peace and security as they focused on themselves instead of God's provision. The beauty of God's holiness was removed. Adam and Eve felt exposed and vulnerable. They attempted to cover their disobedience and shame.

"Then the eyes of both of them were opened, and they knew that they were naked; and they sewed fig leaves together and made themselves loin coverings."
(Genesis 3:7 NASB)

King David declared and rejoiced over God's covering him with His nature, His glory, which provided protection, provision, and deliverance. David looked to God as the One who had the ability and desire to restore him to his ordained position and authority as king.

"But Thou, O Lord, art a shield about me, My glory, and the One who lifts my head." (Psalm 3:3 NASB)

The word, *glory*, denotes God's weight, honor, majesty, abundance, and wealth. *Lifting someone's head* refers to God's ability and desire to restore us to our previous position that mankind knew in the Garden of Eden. We can, once again, walk and talk with God in the cool of the day (Genesis 3:8). Once again, we can operate with the authority and dominion that God originally gave to Adam and Eve (Genesis 1:28).

Pay close attention to something noted in Psalm 3:1-2 (NASB): "O LORD, how my adversaries have increased! Many are rising up against me. Many are saying of my soul, 'There is no deliverance for him in God.'"

The Spoken Blessing I: A Spiritual Posture

King David had fled for his life in the face of a rebellious, scheming son, Absalom. At least 20,000 men had aligned themselves with Absalom to war against the king—20,000 people bent on his destruction. That level of opposition grabbed David's attention and focus. But he was willing to refocus his attention and emotion toward the LORD, Jehovah, the Eternal One, and to trust in His protection and deliverance from evil and destruction. Read David's declaration:

> *But you, O LORD, are a shield about me,*
>   *my glory, and the lifter of my head.*
> *I cried aloud to the LORD,*
>   *and he answered me from his holy hill. Selah*
>
> *I lay down and slept;*
>   *I woke again, for the LORD sustained me.*
> *I will not be afraid of many thousands of people*
>   *who have set themselves against me all around.*
>
> *Arise, O LORD!*
>   *Save me, O my God!*
> *For you strike all my enemies on the cheek;*
>   *you break the teeth of the wicked.*
>
> *Salvation belongs to the LORD;*
>   *your blessing be on your people! Selah*
>
> (Psalm 3:3-8 ESV)

If we had read only the first two verses of Psalm 3, we might have concluded that David was totally defeated in his heart and mind. But that was not his *final answer* to the predicament.

David *chose* to shift his focus from the impending threat to the omnipotent God. King David chose to *Selah*, he *paused* to think about the LORD, God Almighty, the Faithful One, His Deliverer. King David regained his *kingly* posture within God's Kingdom and entered His rest.

David moved forward within the provision of God's Salvation and blessing.

What is the Basis for the Spoken Blessing?

Life Application:

We will encounter people who are focusing on their *woes* of life. When you hear about their challenges, you might understand their concerns. Certainly, extend a compassionate heart, but do not encourage them to wallow in their *woes*. Redirect their focus to their Deliverer, their Provider, their Strength, and their Shield.

Draw from the power of God's word and bless them, by declaring:

May the Lord be your Strength and your Salvation. Whom shall you fear? No one!

May you feel the presence and power of Almighty God as He sends His angels to be in charge concerning your ways.

May you always remember that He will never leave you nor forsake you.

May you know, for certain, that God has great plans for you,

not for calamity, but for a future, full of hope.

May He direct your steps along the pathway of life.

May you draw close to Him and He will draw near to you.

In Jesus' Name, Amen.

The Spoken Blessing is based on:

- God's commitment to His creation
- His commitment to His covenant
- His commitment to His name and nature.

"Look unto me, and be ye saved, all the ends of the earth: for I am God, and there is none else." (Isaiah 45:22 KJV)

"Look" means to turn one's face towards something or someone. God instructs the hearer to focus on Him for his or her salvation since He is God, and there is none other to save them.

Turn to Me, and be saved,
all the ends of the earth;
For I am God, and there is no other.

The Spoken Blessing I: A Spiritual Posture

> *I have sworn by Myself,*
>   *the word has gone forth from My mouth in righteousness*
>   *and will not turn back,*
>
> *that to Me every knee will bow,*
>   *every tongue will swear allegiance.*
>
> (Isaiah 45:22-23 NASB)

The meaning of the Hebrew word for *sworn*, *shaba*, gives us insight into the totality and holiness of God's name and nature. *Shaba* means "to be complete [seven], to swear, to confirm with an oath, to pledge allegiance to God with an oath. *Sheba* or *shibah* means *seven*. The number *seven* was sacred. Oaths were confirmed by seven sacrifices, or by seven witnesses, or seven pledges.

Swearing was the giving of one's unbreakable word that he would faithfully perform a promised deed or that he would not harm his partner. God used this human convention on occasion. Since there was no higher authority than Himself, He swore by Himself or by His holiness.

> *By Myself I have sworn, declares the LORD, because you have done this thing, and have not withheld your son, your only son, indeed I will greatly bless you, and I will greatly multiply your seed as the stars of the heavens, and as the sand which is on the seashore; and your seed shall possess the gate of their enemies. And in your seed all the nations of the earth shall be blessed, because you have obeyed My voice.* (Genesis 22:16-18 NASB)

God swore by Himself to bless Abraham and to greatly multiply Abraham's descendants. He added more revelation to His blessing and plan for Abraham's lineage. God indicated that the fulfillment of Abraham's blessing was dependent upon Himself: His nature, His power, and His resources, and was related to Abraham's obedience.

This fact reminds me of the activity of God as noted in Psalm 17:3 (ESV): *"You have tried my heart, you have visited me by night, you have tested me, and you will find nothing; I have purposed that my mouth will not transgress."*

"Visited" refers to an action on the part of God which produces a beneficial result for His people.

What is the Basis for the Spoken Blessing?

This scripture offers me reassurance of God's faithfully working within my life and within the lives of others. When our daughter, Elizabeth, was in middle school, I was impressed by God's Spirit to speak a specific blessing over her for months and months.

"May you be confident of this very thing, that God will complete and perfect the good work He has begun in you until the day of Jesus Christ." (Philippians 1:6)

I was to set the example of trusting God to be interested and *active* within her life. Years later, as a young mother, Elizabeth is confident that God has an answer for her challenges and a creative solution for her dilemmas. If others observe our trust in God through our words and actions, they are more likely to do the same. We, as believers, are constantly being watched. Do we live a life that expresses confidence in our God to be steadfast to His covenant people? Or are our words and actions indicative of *fear*, *doubt*, and *unbelief*?

Sometimes, there are opportunities for correction in someone's outlook. Sometimes, it's mine that needs correcting. A few years ago, I was being stretched beyond my 'comfort zone:' physically, mentally, spiritually, and emotionally. In exasperation, I exclaimed: "There are not enough hours in the day for me to do ALL that I have to do!" Just as thunder rumbles loudly across the sky, God's voice vibrated within me: "Ann, you have just cursed yourself. You won't have time to do it all because you have bound My hand from helping you. You have limited My blessing you. Take your eyes off of yourself and your circumstances and place them on Me and My abundant provision." It didn't take long for me to repent, to call those word curses *null and void* and to confess God's blessings: supplying all my needs according to His riches in glory through Christ Jesus! (Philippians 4:19)

Years ago, one of our sons was preparing for the GRE (Graduate Record Exam) and asked me to pray. He spoke this declaration about this test: "The outcome of this exam will determine my future!" My response to that was: "No, a test does not determine your future; God does." Then, I followed that correction with a blessing:

May the Lord cause you to prosper and excel in all that you do.
May His Spirit highlight those things that you need to know.

> *May He bring to your remembrance all the facts, figures, and formulas that are needed to complete this test.*
>
> *May the peace of our Lord Jesus guard your heart and your mind.*
>
> *May you call upon Him and He will answer you.*
>
> *In Jesus' Name, Amen.*

The preceding blessing is explained in the Life Application.

Life Application:

If you were to search the Scriptures for that specific blessing, you would not find it. Many times, I base my blessings on the principles found within God's word and on the character and operation of the Holy Trinity. I know that God desires for us to "prosper and excel" in all that we do because I have read the story about Joseph as he served Potiphar, an Egyptian officer of Pharaoh (Genesis 39:1-6 NASB):

> *Now Joseph had been taken down to Egypt; and Potiphar, an Egyptian officer of Pharaoh, the captain of the bodyguard, bought him from the Ishmaelites, who had taken him down there. And the LORD was with Joseph, so he became a successful man. And he was in the house of his master, the Egyptian. Now his master saw that the LORD was with him and how the LORD caused all that he did to prosper in his hand. So Joseph found favor in his sight, and became his personal servant; and he made him overseer over his house, and all that he owned he put in his charge. And it came about that from the time he made him overseer in his house, and over all that he owned, the LORD blessed the Egyptian's house on account of Joseph; thus the LORD's blessing was upon all that he owned, in the house and in the field. So he left everything he owned in Joseph's charge; and with him there he did not concern himself with anything, except the food which he ate.*

I assimilated that principle of God's blessing His people into my perception of Him and His activity. Secondly, as I have grown in my understanding and experience with God's Spirit, I have recognized the consistent way He teaches, trains, informs, and reminds me of things I need to know and do. This agrees with the scripture in which Jesus explained the promise and the purpose of His Spirit.

> *But the Helper, the Holy Spirit, whom the Father will send in My name, He will teach you all things, and bring to your remembrance all that I said to you. Peace I leave with you; My peace I give to you; not as the world gives, do I give to you. Let not your heart be troubled, nor let it be fearful.* (John 14:26-27 NASB)

God honors His word to people. He upholds His integrity and honor by performing whatever He agreed to within a covenant. We do have a *better covenant* with God through His Son, Jesus Christ. Remember: God operated within a human custom as He swore by Himself to fulfill His promise to Abraham, to give us strong encouragement and hope in Him and in the unchangeableness of His purpose (Hebrews 6:13-19). Through God, we can expect to obtain every good thing. We can help others in grasping and applying this hope, this assurance of God's faithfulness to them, as we speak blessings into their lives.

His truth must become the anchor of their soul.

Holy Spirit directed me to write a set of blessings entitled: *Hope: The Anchor of the Soul*©. He impressed me with people's deep need for *hope*. Remember, *hope* refers to a desire for a good thing with the expectation of obtaining it. He showed me that many people, including myself, have grown up hearing: "Well, honey, I don't want you to get your hopes up." People have said that to me throughout my life, under the pretense of comforting me. But it did the opposite. I lost hope for a better future. Honestly, that statement undermines one's ability to expect their desire to be fulfilled. It is counterproductive to true *hope*.

Many have dared to hope for something and have been disappointed and hurt because their focus and expectation was placed on the wrong source. Our focus must be redirected to God. He is the Supplier of every need. He is our Good Shepherd; we shall have no want (Psalm 23:1).

I bless others with *hope* that their faithful God will supply all their needs according to His riches in glory in Christ Jesus (Philippians 4:19). In my blessing, I remind them that God is able to make all grace abound to them, having all sufficiency in everything, enabling them to accomplish every good work (II Corinthians 9:8). Do you see how *hope* can be built and encouraged as you release such a blessing?!

That blessing of hope and encouragement can flow both ways. We can sow blessings into the soil of another's heart and personally reap God's benefits.

II Corinthians 9:10-11 (NASB) explains:

Now He who supplies seed to the sower and bread for food, will supply and multiply your seed for sowing and increase the harvest of your righteousness; you will be enriched in everything for all liberality, which is producing thanksgiving to God.

Notice several consequences of sowing seeds of God's blessings:

1. The harvest of your righteousness will be increased (indicating success in being fruitful and multiplying).

Personally, I have received many testimonies of how *the Spoken Blessing* has impacted people's lives: their confidence has been revived, their friends have accepted Jesus as their Savior, thoughts of suicide have been overcome, negative attitudes have been exchanged for an excitement for life and expectations for good things to happen.

Cal and I are observing, with great delight and awe, how God has multiplied and nurtured the seeds of compassion and generosity that have been sown within our four children. As adults our children express God's compassion and help in different ways, yet their 'fruit' is recognizable. God continues to provide Cal and me with more opportunities; more seed for sowing His blessings.

2. Your liberality and good deeds will be enhanced and increased because you have been enriched.

Cal and I always ask God to increase our abilities and wisdom as we serve others.

Yes, God is more than ready to overwhelm you with every form of grace, so that you will have more than enough of everything---every moment and in every way. He will make you overflow with abundance in every good thing you do.

You will be abundantly enriched in every way as you give generously on every occasion, for when we take your gifts to those in need, it causes many to give thanks to God. (II Corinthians 9:8,11 TPT)

3. Others will offer thanksgiving to God because of your liberality and good deeds.

As we bless others, their focus is directed to God and to trusting and thanking Him "to do exceedingly abundantly beyond all that they ask or think, according to the power that works within them" (Ephesians 3:20).

"The priestly ministry you are providing through your offering not only supplies what is lacking for God's people, it inspires an outpouring of praises and thanksgiving to God himself." (II Corinthians 9:12 TPT)

The blessing of God is eternal. His commitment to His creation, His covenant, His holy name and nature, is forever and everlasting. This foundational truth must sink down into your soul: your mind, will, and emotions. This understanding is vital to your ability and confidence in speaking and receiving *the Spoken Blessing*. Speak and release a blessing over someone today.

This is my blessing for you:
May you know God as the great, I AM.
May He become everything to you.
May you love Him with all your heart, soul, mind, and strength.
May you love your neighbor as yourself.
May you look for opportunities to bless others.
May God's Holy Spirit give you boldness to declare His word over others.
May they receive the Spoken Blessing with joy and hope for their future.
May you give thanksgiving to God for His steadfast love.
In Jesus' Name, Amen.

Journal of My Journey with the Spoken Blessing

I am confident that God wants to bless His creation because ...

_____
_____
_____

I know God as a "covenant-keeping" God by His ...

_____
_____
_____

I am not adequate by myself to bless others, but with ...

_____
_____
_____

I will help to redirect someone's focus back to God by ...

_____
_____
_____

What is the Basis for the Spoken Blessing?

I have witnessed God's activity in my life when He ...

_____

_____

_____

Write a blessing for someone who is struggling with a situation.

_____

_____

_____

_____

"Anxiety in the heart of man weighs it down, But a good word makes it glad." (Proverbs 12:25 NASB)

Chapter Three
When is the Spoken Blessing Given?

Most of us recognize the importance of *timing* within the natural and supernatural worlds. The saying goes: "Timing is everything." Young children learn when not to interrupt Daddy's activity and when to obey Mommy as they get that "look" from her. Throughout our daily lives, *timing* is essential to accomplish our tasks. As we prepare a gift, we carefully consider *when* to give it.

Ecclesiastes 3:1 identifies: *"To everything there is a season, and a time to every purpose under the heaven:"* (KJV)

Season stems from a word that means: *to be determined, to be appointed, to be fixed*. It refers to an appointed time or times. *Time* relates to the *right time*, the *proper time*, a *season*, or a *short-lived season*. There are three principal situations which the word, *time,* describes:

1. regular events
2. the appropriate time for a nonrecurring incident
3. a set time

The Greek equivalent for *time* used in the New Testament is *kairos*. *Kairos* implies that which *time gives an opportunity to do*. It implies not the convenience of the season, but the necessity of the *task at hand*—whether the time provides a good, convenient opportunity or not.

Purpose signifies *pleasure, delight, wish, desire,* a *matter, business,* or *pursuit*.

Isaiah 53:10 states that God's delight or good pleasure will prosper in the hand of the Messiah.

Will God's *purpose* prosper in our hands?

Our spiritual posture, at this point, is one of submission.

We must ask our Father's pleasure and desire as we prepare to bless others. What does He want to accomplish in that person's life? What pursuit can we encourage as we release blessings into their life? Our spiritual posture, at this point, is one of submission. This type of submission is depicted in the familiar pictures of Jesus sitting on the ground next to a large rock. His hands are clasped, resting on the rock---His eyes and face are focused on the heavens. *Jesus constantly submitted Himself to His Father*, asking for His will to be made known. Then, in obedience, He responded (Luke 6:12-13). We must ask Holy Spirit to bring to our remembrance the words of Christ that will reflect His will.

Recall in Genesis 49:28, what is said concerning the blessing of Jacob's sons: *"He blessed them, every one with the blessing appropriate to him."* As we are the Lord's representatives, we must be sensitive to His timing and purpose for releasing a Spoken Blessing. There is a task at hand to be accomplished: *"We are ambassadors for Christ, as though God were entreating through us; we beg you on behalf of Christ, be reconciled to God."*
(II Corinthians 5:20 NASB)

Our task is assisting in the reconciliation and restoration of people *to* God through introducing them *to* Christ or to readjusting their focus to Christ. *The Spoken Blessing* is a tool we can use to accomplish this task. There will be occasions when you feel the need to correct or redirect someone as you bless them:

> *May you not continue to call this day 'bad,' but call it 'good,' for God's word says:*
>
> *'This is the day that the Lord has made, I will rejoice and be glad in it.'*

When is the Spoken Blessing Given?

May you not look upon your days with sorrow, but with joy, rejoicing that the Lord has declared that He will never leave you nor forsake you."

As you speak this blessing, the hearer will likely assume an attitude of repentance. They may nod their heads or verbally respond: "Yes, Lord. I'm sorry. It is a good day." You would continue to bless them:

May you gain wisdom from your past and approach your future with a new attitude and outlook. May your eyes be focused on the author and finisher of your faith, Lord Jesus.

May you focus your face like flint on Him as He beckons you to walk on the water; to step out of your comfort zone, relying totally on Him.

May you not lean on your own understanding, but trust in Him.

In Jesus' Name, Amen.

In that blessing, you have presented them with a need for repentance by speaking the truth of God's word in love. You have redirected their thoughts to the God's truth which will liberate and edify them. You have encouraged them to submit their lives and future to the authority and faithfulness of our Lord Jesus. In essence, you have accomplished the task at hand. In doing so, you have followed the example of Jesus found in Matthew 4:17 (AMP):

From that time Jesus began to preach, crying out Repent [change your mind for the better, heartily amend your ways, with abhorrence of your past sins], for the kingdom of heaven is at hand.

The kingdom of heaven and *the kingdom of God* are interchangeable phrases. Spiritually, the kingdom of God is within the human heart; within the heart that has been humbled and receptive to God's authority and control. There was a specific timing when Jesus introduced the kingdom of heaven. John the Baptist had been imprisoned. He had prepared the way for Jesus' public ministry to begin.

Consider the definition of *heaven*: aloft, the sky, height, heaven(s). There are two main categories:

1. the physical heavens with differing locations
2. where God lives

The Spoken Blessing can address the physical world and the spiritual world. I have spoken this blessing over our adult sons when they played softball:

> *"May God give you the strength to run, the discernment for which ball to hit and the accuracy to 'field' the ball.*
>
> *May His angels be set in charge concerning all your ways.*
>
> *May your conduct be such as to glorify your heavenly Father.*
>
> *May you have victory.*
>
> *In Jesus' Name, Amen."*

Is it wrong to bless others in such ordinary events such as playing softball? No! God desires for us to prosper and excel in *all* that we do! God set the example for us as I discussed in Chapter 2. Let's review Genesis 39:3 (NASB): *"Now his master saw that the LORD was with him and how the LORD caused all that he did to prosper in his hand."*

Heaven's supernatural touch reached Earth for supernatural purposes.

The tasks that Joseph accomplished for Potiphar were in the natural, physical realm. Yet, Heaven touched Earth for supernatural purposes. The Lord's perfect *timing* is emphasized throughout the story of Joseph being sold into slavery, purchased by Potiphar, used and abused as a slave, then promoted to a position of great authority, power, and influence. Joseph gained respect from unbelievers.

Speaking of *time,* we must commit ourselves to take the *time* to speak blessings into people's lives. Be alert to the events in people's lives which cause them stress, concern, joy, and excitement. Be sensitive and responsive to their specific interests. As you personalize a blessing to their need, they will listen and receive it. The potential of our sons' *softball playing* blessing was that it:

> 1. Reinforced that God was so personal that He was interested in the *little* things that were significant to them.

> Our Big, Big God is sincerely interested in the extremely small details of our lives.

2. Focused their attention to "from whence cometh my help." God would be acknowledged as they succeed in their sport.

"I will lift up my eyes to the mountains; from whence shall my help come? My help comes from the LORD, who made heaven and earth."
(Psalm 121:1,2 NASB)

3. Provided an opportunity to tell others about God's favor and grace that surrounded them.

Anthony, our eldest son, was injured on the softball field. Painfully lying on the ground, he testified to a friend about God's miraculous healing of his heart when he was seven and that he trusted God to heal him again. Our friend was deeply touched by God's mercy and, subsequently, honored God as she shared her own testimony of the Lord's healing power. What the enemy meant for harm, God turned it for good.

His healing mercies were remembered and honored.

Anthony's back was restored within two weeks.

He was victorious through Christ!

4. Drew attention of others towards the Lord's favor (Genesis 39:3).

As our friend described the circumstances concerning Anthony's softball injury, she honored the Lord for all that He had done in our lives, recognizing His steadfast favor that rested upon us.

5. Encouraged me in my faith, that God cares for my children and assists them in all their ways:

"So faith comes from hearing and hearing by the word of Christ."
(Romans 10:17 NASB)

God reassured me that when I can't be there for my children, especially in a time of need, He will send someone to assist them. Our friend was there to pray for and comfort Anthony.

Softball games are *regular events* in the context of the definition of *time*. Let's consider other *regular events*:

The Spoken Blessing in Other "Regular Events"

1. Attending school: Relationships, reports, tests, try-outs, etc., can be blessed.

Consider the principle described in Proverbs 20:11 (NASB): *"It is by his deeds that a lad distinguishes himself if his conduct is pure and right."*

and translate it into a Spoken Blessing:

"May your thoughts, actions, and words be pure and right. May they set you apart from others."

Consider Daniel 1:17 (NASB):

"And as for these four youths, God gave them knowledge and intelligence in every branch of literature and wisdom; Daniel even understood all kinds of visions and dreams."

and compose a blessing with it:

May God give you wisdom, knowledge, and understanding in every area of your education.
May He give you revelation in visions, dreams, and in the supernatural.
May you always give God the glory for your abilities.
In Jesus' Name, Amen.

In Daniel 2:19-23 (NASB), carefully read Daniel's response to God after He had honored his request for help:

Then the mystery was revealed to Daniel in a night vision. Then Daniel blessed the God of heaven;
Daniel answered and said,
"Let the name of God be blessed forever and ever, for wisdom and power belong to Him.
And it is He who changes the times and the epochs;
He removes kings and establishes kings; He gives wisdom to wise men, and knowledge to men of understanding.

It is He who reveals the profound and hidden things;
He knows what is in the darkness, and the light dwells with Him.
To Thee, O God of my fathers, I give thanks and praise, for Thou hast given me wisdom and power; even now Thou hast made known to me what we requested of Thee, for Thou hast made known to us the king's matter."

Encouraging this submissive and awe-filled attitude towards God is a primary goal of releasing the blessing over people.

The fact that Daniel blessed the name of God is noteworthy. It indicates a humble attitude, one filled with respect, submission, and recognition of God's supreme dominion and authority over Daniel's life and over those around him. Encouraging this submissive and awe-filled attitude towards God is a primary goal of releasing the blessing over people. When the cares of life challenge people, we can direct their focus to the One who knows everything and has an answer for all situations. We can help build their confidence to the level that Daniel possessed.

Meditating or thinking about God's goodness and mercy is an important spiritual activity to develop.

Daniel blessed the name of the Lord. We can set this example as we ask our children how the Lord worked good things in their day. Meditating or thinking about God's goodness and mercy is an important spiritual activity to develop. When your children describe God's activity in their lives, begin to bless Him for being their Provider, their Healer, their Protector, and their Faithful Friend. This should be an ongoing process of learning how to honor God, His nature, and His name. Cultivating an attitude of gratitude is foundational in developing our relationship with God.

When I pray and bless people at our church, I ask them to later share with me how God responded to their need. Many do. Together, we glorify God and thank Him for His loving-kindness. We are both encouraged *to not grow weary of doing well* (Galatians 6:9).

Our praise and thanksgiving sanctify God in our lives. We set Him apart as the One to receive *all* honor and glory!

Relationships can be blessed:

May the Lord provide a friend for you as He did for Jonathan and David.

May your friendship be based on love and commitment, preferring the other over yourself.

May you serve to encourage one another.

May you uphold and honor the reputation of each other.

May you, both, be upright and faithful to the Lord.

(I Samuel 19:1-7; 20:1-23)

I would encourage you to read I Samuel 19 and 20. Consider the dynamics of the situation and the unselfish love that was shown.

Jonathan spoke a blessing over David in 1 Samuel 20:13.

2. Working 9 to 5: This *regular event* encompasses a majority of the adult population.

One of my favorite blessings to speak over fellow believers is found in Ruth 2:12 (NASB): *"May the LORD reward your work, and your wages be full from the LORD, the God of Israel, under whose wings you have come to seek refuge."*

Remember that Deuteronomy 28 identifies the extensiveness of God's blessings for His people. This includes our careers and working environment: *"Blessed shall you be in the city, and blessed shall you be in the country."* (Deuteronomy 28:3 NASB)

Deuteronomy 8:18 (NASB) reminds us that God is committed to upholding His covenant, which translates into financially supporting and strengthening His people: *"But you shall remember the LORD your*

When is the Spoken Blessing Given?

God, for it is He who is giving you power to make wealth, that He may confirm His covenant which He swore to your fathers, as it is this day."

Using this verse and foundational truth, a blessing can be spoken:

May you always remember the LORD your God, for it is He who gives you power to make wealth. May His faithfulness to you confirm His covenant that He established with His people over the generations.

In Jesus' Name, Amen."

The strength of generations is anchored in God's faithfulness to His nature and character. He is committed to His creation and His covenant. He upholds His name and nature. We are to declare the truths that are in God's word. Here's another blessing concerning *wealth* or money:

May you bring the whole tithe into the storehouse, so that there may be food in God's house.

May you prove to yourself that God is true to His word, that as you give Him a tenth of all your earnings, you will see Him open the windows of heaven and pour out for you a blessing until it overflows.

May you know the LORD as your Good Shepherd, for you shall have no want.

In Jesus' Name, Amen. (Malachi 3:10; Psalm 23:1)

We are to request and accept the *whole* counsel of the LORD, Jehovah, the Self-Existent One. We are not to *cut and paste* the verses we like, discarding those that challenge us or correct us. Tithing, returning to the LORD a tenth of our total earnings, is vital to our experiencing the fullness of God's blessings. Being faithful to give gifts and offerings is a component part of our being generous. As we give to others, we are giving to the Him. He declared it:

Then the righteous will answer Him, saying, Lord, when did we see You hungry, and feed You, or thirsty, and give You drink? And when did we see You a stranger, and invite You in, or naked, and clothe You? And when did we see You sick, or in prison, and come to You? And the King will answer and say to them, Truly I say to you, to the extent that you did it to one of these brothers of Mine, even the least of them, you did it to Me. (Matthew 25:37-40 NASB)

We are to receive God's word for our own lives and impart His truths to others. We can do this through using *the Spoken Blessing*. Our faith should not be expressed only in our traditional Sunday worship services. Our faith should be seen within our daily lives in the way we conduct ourselves and in how we relate to others: our God, our family, our co-workers, and our neighbors. The book of Ruth provides several excellent examples of people living out their faith in the presence of others.

In Ruth 1:4, we discover that Naomi lived with her two sons and their Moabite wives for ten years in the land of Moab. After the death of both sons, Naomi decided to return to Bethlehem, accompanied by her two daughters-in-law. In Ruth 1:8-9 (NASB), Naomi encouraged these women to return to Moab and spoke a blessing over them, calling upon the covenant name of God to bless them: *"May the LORD deal kindly with you as you have dealt with the dead and with me. May the LORD grant that you may find rest, each in the house of her husband."*

Naomi would not have used the name of God if she knew her daughters-in-law would not have recognized nor understood it. When we speak to someone, we employ words and terms that they understand. The purpose of communication is to receive, impart and exchange information. Therefore, it would be safe to assume that Naomi had lived a life of faith before her daughters-in-law during those ten years. Ruth 1:16-17 (NASB) identifies the positive influence her faith had on one of these women.

But Ruth said, "Do not urge me to leave you or turn back from following you; for where you go, I will go, and where you lodge, I will lodge. Your people shall be my people, and your God, my God. Where you die, I will die, and there I will be buried. Thus may the LORD do to me and worse, if anything but death parts you and me."

Your life touches others.

Walking out our faith, day after day, can have a similar influence on people. During the 40 or more hours each week that you spend at work, you have great potential for imparting your faith to others. You can release blessings over people within your work environment as Boaz did in his: *"Now behold, Boaz came from Bethlehem and said to the reapers, 'May the LORD be with you.' And they said to him, 'May the LORD bless you.'"* (Ruth 2:4)

Cal and I owned and operated a retail business in Tallahassee, Florida. Within our store, we took the liberty to pray for and bless our customers. Our employees exercised the same liberty. It was not unusual for our customers to return and share how God moved on their behalf. We had the privilege of celebrating with them, thanking God for His mercy and grace.

You have a sphere of influence whether your work is within your home, or within the classroom of your child (as a volunteer), within your neighborhood, your business, your recreational activities, etc. Your life touches others. What impact will you have on them?

3. Attending weekly worship services:

Every believer has a responsibility to edify and build up one another.

We are to be equipped *"for the work of service, to the building up of the body of Christ."*
WHEN and for HOW LONG...

"Until we all attain to the unity of the faith, and of the knowledge of the Son of God, to a mature man, to the measure of the stature which belongs to the fullness of Christ." (Ephesians 4:12-13 NASB)

Speaking blessings over fellow believers can help accomplish this. Many Christians embrace negative attitudes about themselves, their future, and others. God's word explains the power of possessing a dream or vision for our future because *"where there is no vision, the people perish"* (Proverbs 29:18 KJV). When we release the power of God's life-changing word, their lives will be transformed; their minds will be renewed (Romans 12:2).

God has given us the ministry of reconciliation and committed to us the word of reconciliation (II Corinthians 5:18-19). On many occasions, I have witnessed a positive reaction within people when I speak a blessing over them and close with, "In Jesus' Name." With a change in their countenance, they smile and say, "Thank you." Our spirits connect through our eyes. This simple exchange often provides a platform for further discussion of the Lord, His support, and His love for them. God continues to *awe* me as I watch Him touch and transform others through His powerful word.

If you hear someone expressing doubt about their abilities, their future, or even, disappointments with their past, you could speak a blessing filled with God's truth to combat the lies that are echoing in their mind and heart.

May you always remember that before you were in your mother's womb, God knew you. Before you were born, God consecrated you, setting you aside for His holy purposes. He has appointed you to do great and mighty things for His kingdom. May you trust in God's word as He declared that His plans for you are for peace and not evil, to give you a future and a hope. (Jeremiah 1:5; 29:11)

You may hear a Sunday School teacher express their discouragement or frustration with a situation or person (that does happen even in the best churches). Encourage them with this blessing:

May you not lose heart in doing good, for in due time you will reap if you do not grow weary. May you be assured that God is not unjust so as to forget your work and the love you have shown toward His name, in having ministered and in still ministering to the... {children, adults, teens}. (Galatians 6:9; Hebrews 6:10)

Someone else needs to be blessed during our worship services, at work, at home, and at play:

"I will extol Thee, my God, O King; and I will bless Thy name forever and ever. Every day I will bless Thee, And I will praise Thy name forever and ever." (Psalm 145:1-2 NASB)

Every day, we shall express our adoration and gratitude to our God, our King.

When is the Spoken Blessing Given?

Every day, we shall lift His name above every name, confessing His Lordship over our lives.

Every day, we shall praise His works and declare His mighty acts to others.

Every day, His godly ones shall bless Him.

As our focus remains on Him, we shall gain strength and shall be renewed in our inner beings to accomplish all that God has commanded us. How can we lose? How can we feel defeated when we remain focused on our God, who He is to us and to His world? As we bless the Lord, every day, our confidence will increase and become solidified as a foundation in our lives. It is from this strong assurance in God that we feel confident in speaking His blessings to others.

Let's consider our final example of *regular events* for blessing others:

4. Caring for a child:

Cal and I began blessing our youngest child, before we discovered that I was pregnant with him. {I will discuss this in Chapter 7.} Therefore, it was only natural for me to continue to bless David once he arrived. After his morning bath, I applied baby lotion to different parts of his body. As I moved from one area to another, I blessed him using the familiar "Armor of God" passage found in Ephesians 6: *"May you put on the Helmet of Salvation, knowing Jesus as your personal Savior."*

{As a three-year-old, David invited Jesus to touch his heart. Two years later, in a children's service, David accepted Jesus as his Savior. As a child's understanding of Jesus develops, he may feel a need to repeat his confession of belief in Jesus.}

I continued to apply lotion as I moved across his little body:

"May you always wear the Breastplate of Righteousness. May you love the Lord, your God, with all your heart, and with all your soul, and with all your mind." (Matthew 22:37)

As I was completing this part, Holy Spirit spoke to me, instructing me to finish that blessing. I paused, then realized what He meant. I continued with the passage in Matthew 22:39: *"May you love your neighbor as yourself."*

At that time, David was a few months old. I did not understand the significance of including that part, but I obeyed. I trusted that God knew David's future and the *purpose under heaven* for David's life.

Four years later, I was preparing to speak for a ladies' conference. Holy Spirit directed me to a scripture, then opened my heart and eyes as to the reason behind David's blessing:

A new commandment I give to you, that you love one another, even as I have loved you, that you also love one another: By this all men will know that you are My disciples, if you have love for one another. (John 13:34-35 NASB)

By relating this scripture to David's blessing, Holy Spirit allowed me to peer into David's destiny. That one glance motivated me to continue speaking blessings which encouraged David's love and compassion for others.

"David, may you be kind to others, tender-hearted, forgiving others, just as God in Christ has forgiven you." (Ephesians 4:32)

Today David is known for his kindness, compassion and willingness to forgive. His name describes who he is: *Beloved*.

Even if you don't fully understand the depth and magnitude of the blessing, follow the Spirit's leading.

When is *the Spoken Blessing* given? Anytime God's Spirit prompts you to bless, do so. His Spirit knows what a person needs and when they need it. When God's Spirit prompts you, obey. Even if you don't fully understand the depth and magnitude of the blessing, follow the Spirit's leading. Remember, God's ways and thoughts are higher and greater than ours (Isaiah 55:9). We simply want to agree with His ways, causing them to prosper in our hearts, hands, and mouths.

We can bless others at the appropriate time for *nonrecurring events*. Usually, you have time to prepare a blessing for these specific occasions. As God's word declares: Jesus sits at the right hand of the Father, interceding on our behalf (Romans 8:34; Hebrews 7:25). Before the Father, Jesus presents us as those who have believed in Him and accepted His forgiveness of sin through His blood. Understanding the frailty of our humanity, Jesus entreats the Father for His mercy. As our Good Shepherd, Jesus prepares the way for our needs to be met. You and I can prepare blessings for special occasions, knowing the individuals and anticipating their needs.

Nonrecurring Occasions to Bless Others with a Spoken Blessing

1. High school prom or graduation.

Many parents of teenagers become concerned for their safety as Prom Night and Graduation approach. Many of us have read tragic stories that have occurred on those specific nights. Too many teenagers have lost their lives or their budding futures to accidents that have happened during those celebrations. We have a great opportunity to pray and bless our children before they leave on these special evenings.

On the night of our second son's prom, I was busily preparing dinner for the family. Into the kitchen strolled Peyton, looking quite handsome in his tuxedo. He made this mama proud! Do you know what he said? "Mama, will you bless me?" I wanted to cry. Even as I spoke a blessing, I struggled not to weep. This was the son I described in the Preface of this book, *Sharing Shadows*. This time, my tearfulness was not from anguish, but from gratitude and delight. I was grateful to God for the transformation that had occurred within Peyton. I was proud of our son for excelling and making good choices within his life.

A portion of Peyton's blessing follows:

May you dwell in the shelter of the Most High. May you abide in the shadow of the Almighty. May you make the Lord your refuge. May no evil befall you. May He give His angels charge concerning you, to guard you in all your ways. Because you have loved Him, may the Lord deliver you and set you securely on high. (Psalm 91:1,10,11,14)

2. Marriage

In Chapter 1, we read Rebekah's blessing that was spoken over her by her family as she prepared to leave. We discussed how Rebekah carried this blessing into her marriage with Isaac, who also added a blessing to their union.

Think about what you would like to see happen within someone's marriage: love for the Lord, love for each other, children, peace, prosperity, provision, satisfaction, etc. Grab your Bible and turn to its Concordance. I also use *The New Strong's Exhaustive Concordance of the Bible*. Look up different topics and their references. Locate the passages and principles identified in those scriptures. Write them in the format: *"May the Lord..."* or *"May you..."*

The reason we use the word, *may*, is that the Hebrew language has two verb tenses: past and present/future. The English language has three verb tenses: past, present, and future. Our word, *may*, is used to convey the Hebrew verb tense---present/future.

May your focus be on the Lord as you trust in Him, and He will keep you in perfect peace. May God grant you His wisdom upon which you will build your house. May He give you understanding in all things which will become the foundation of your home. May the knowledge of Him and His ways fill your rooms with all precious and pleasant riches. May you not neglect doing good and sharing, for with such sacrifices God is pleased. May God equip you in every good thing to do His will, working in you that which is pleasing in His sight. (Isaiah 26:3; Proverbs 24:3,4; Hebrews 13:16,21)

Another key issue in the timing of *the Spoken Blessing* is indicated in (Proverbs 3:27-28 NASB):

Do not withhold good from those to whom it is due, When it is in your power to do it.
Do not say to your neighbor, "Go, and come back, And tomorrow I will give it." When you have it with you."

"When" is then.

When someone asks you to pray for them, or to bless them, don't hesitate. Do it, then. "When" is then. Remember, the definition of *kairos* implies not the convenience of the season, but the necessity of the *task at hand*, whether the time provides a good, convenient opportunity or not. Too many times, I have agreed to pray for someone, then walked away and forgotten to do it. Now, I make every effort to pray and bless them, right then! People are always grateful that I take the time, right then. God's peace enters and His Spirit directs my words. The recipient leaves filled with reassurance of God's love and purpose for them. They depart richer than they came; more determined to be victorious. I feel encouraged and grateful when God uses me.

Set Times

The final definition of *time* is a *set time*. This reminds me of a scheduled or planned event, one for which you have time to prepare a blessing.

Some of those *set times* might be: a baby shower, bridal shower, 'going away' party, 50th birthday party, or a retirement party. Before you begin writing, ask God how He would like to bless this person. Ask Him what He desires to activate, stimulate, or renew within their life. Consider the circumstances surrounding them. Carefully consider and meditate on God's word, reflecting on the *time or season* of this person's life. (Proverbs 25:11 NASB) explains: *"Like apples of gold in settings of silver is a word spoken in right circumstances."*

Adorn your friend with the beauty of the Lord by releasing God's word over their life.

Imagine the beauty of the Scriptures being gracefully draped about that person's neck as silver entwined with gold. The silver of redemption, blended with the gold of divinity, produces a magnificent picture of our Lord Jesus. The Lord's delight and purpose is for the redemption and restoration of His creation, restoring the divine image of their original being. Adorn your friend with the beauty of the Lord by releasing God's word over their life. Declare God's desire by releasing a Spoken Blessing over the lives of others.

The Spoken Blessing I: A Spiritual Posture

May I do the same for you:

May you always remember that God's love for you has no beginning and no end, for it is everlasting, forever and ever.

May you feel His strong arm supporting you and His faithful love strengthening you.

May you recognize His favor operating within your life.

May you see His hand of provision, meeting your every need.

May you learn to trust in the timeliness of His answers.

May you draw near to Him, seeking His understanding for your dilemmas.

May His Spirit bring to your remembrance the words of Christ, giving you instruction and direction for your path of life.

May you rest in Him.

In Jesus' Name, Amen.

Journal of My Journey with the Spoken Blessing

When someone asks me to pray for them, I usually:
___
___
___

I will change my response to them by:
___
___
___

God's purposes will prosper in my hands as I:
___
___
___

The scriptures that strengthen my confidence in speaking a blessing are:
___
___
___

The Spoken Blessing I: A Spiritual Posture

Write a blessing to honor the Lord.

_____

_____

_____

_____

Write a blessing pertaining to someone's business or career.

_____

_____

_____

_____

"The generous man will be prosperous, and he who waters will himself be watered." (Proverbs 11:25 NASB)

Chapter Four

Where Must We Be Spiritually to Bless Others?

- Where must we be in our relationship with God?
- What must happen within our hearts and minds to enable us to bless others?
- What truths, found in the God's word, must be grounded within our inner being?

"Forever, O LORD, Your word is settled in heaven; Your faithfulness continues throughout all generations; You established the earth, and it stands." (Psalm 119:89-90 NASB)

In Hebrew, the word *settled* is *Natsab*, which means: *to be set up, to be stationed, to station oneself, to stand; to be firm or healthy; to set, to place, to erect, to establish. It portrays various types of standing, waiting, and postures. It means to be in a position of authority.*

Is God's word *settled* as the authority in our lives? Have we erected any mind sets or predispositions which are contrary to His word? What attitudes and precepts must prevail to allow us the freedom to bless and not curse? I Peter 3:8-9 (NASB) answers that question:

> *To sum up, let all be harmonious, sympathetic, brotherly, kindhearted, and humble in spirit; not returning evil for evil, or insult for*

> *insult, but giving a blessing instead; for you were called for the very purpose that you might inherit a blessing.*

Verse 8 indicates that we *all* should be harmonious, sympathetic, etc. Is there even *one* of us who could truthfully say that we possess *all* those wonderful qualities to the fullest degree? These verses serve as a standard by which we judge ourselves. They set the goal for which we strive. What's a person to do? How do we reach that goal?

Consider the analogy described in II Timothy 2:20-22 (NASB):

> *Now in a large house there are not only gold and silver vessels, but also vessels of wood and of earthenware, and some to honor and some to dishonor: Therefore, if a man cleanses himself from these things, he will be a vessel for honor, sanctified, useful to the Master, prepared for every good work. Now flee from youthful lusts, and pursue righteousness, faith, love, and peace, with those who call on the Lord from a pure heart.*

A pure heart closely describes the heart portrayed in (I Peter 3:8-9). How do we develop and maintain a *pure heart*? II Timothy 2:21 (NASB) answers that question: *"If a man cleanses himself from these things."*

And what are *"these things?"* The preceding verses 16 and 19 of II Timothy 2, identify *"these things."*

"But avoid worldly and empty chatter, for it will lead to further ungodliness,"

"Let everyone who names the name of the Lord abstain from wickedness."

The King James Version of verse 16 reads:

"But shun profane and vain babblings: for they will increase unto more ungodliness."

Anything that is *profane* is *void of religion and piety*. When this word is applied to a person, it indicates a lack of all *affinity* to God. *Affinity* refers to a *close relationship, connection, a similarity in structure and nature*. Thus, within a profane person or within their speech, there is no resemblance to the character and nature of God.

Webster's Dictionary explained *chatter* as *rapid, foolish talk*, whereas the definition of *babblings* is *foolish or meaningless talk; a continuous mur-*

mur. To add fuel to this ugly fire of speech, Timothy used the descriptive word: *vain*. Timothy identified that this *meaningless talk* was *fruitless speaking, devoid of any divine or spiritual character*. This type of speech offered nothing to the shaping and molding of the Christian life and character. He related this to an increasing lack of reverence toward God, and to disrespect for oneself and others.

How can these wicked murmurings *increase* ungodliness? Numbers 13 notes that the Lord directed Moses to send twelve spies to investigate the land of Canaan. This was the same land God had given to Abraham for him and his descendants (Genesis 12:6-8). This was the land *flowing with milk and honey* that God confirmed ownership to Moses in Exodus 3:6-8. It was no surprise to Moses for God to give him such instructions as found in Numbers 13. Spying out the land of Canaan was simply the next step towards fulfilling God's ordained plan for His people.

When these twelve spies returned with their report of the land, they answered many of the questions Moses posed in verses 18-20. Their description of the inhabitants and their cities obviously disturbed the Israelites, for Caleb *"quieted the people before Moses"* (Numbers 13:30). As an expression of his faith in God and to reassure the congregation, Caleb said, *"We should by all means go up and take possession of it, for we shall surely overcome it."* Faith in God, that was resident within him, rose up and was released by Caleb's confession.

Yet somewhere along the way, ten spies had forsaken their confidence in God, had forgotten *all* that God had done for them in Egypt and in their exodus. Those ten spies walked about Canaan and discarded God's word which declared that land to be His promise to them: His inheritance for them. As those ten, tribal leaders surveyed the land, inquired about the people, and investigated the cities; they chose to embrace an attitude of *fear, doubt,* and *unbelief*. Canaan is a symbol of inheritance gained by warfare. The number forty is symbolic of probation and testing, which ends in victory or defeat. Ten spies were defeated in their faith; two spies were victorious champions in their faith. The number two is symbolic of being a witness, giving a testimony or being divided or separated. Joshua and Caleb bore witness to the supremacy of God's directive and His power to fulfill His promise. Choosing to stand with God, these two valiant warriors separated themselves from *fear, doubt* and *unbelief*.[1]

---

1   Interpreting the Symbols and Types, by Kevin J. Conner, pp. 133,144,176

Do we choose to live in victory or defeat?

Can we learn from their mistakes? Consider the areas that tested the spies' faith: land, people, and cities. What is our attitude about the geographical location in which we live? Do we call it blessed or cursed? How do we view the people that live, work, and recreate with or around us? How do we interact with them? Do we speak well of our neighbors and neighborhoods, or do we judge them and our community? How do we speak about fellow believers? Do we recognize their weaknesses and not their strengths? Is your city being blessed by your words; do you support the officials or condemn them?

"By the blessing of the upright a city is exalted, but by the mouth of the wicked it is torn down." (Proverbs 11:11 NASB)

Do we choose to live in victory or defeat?

Consider what happened because of the defeated attitudes of the ten spies.

"So they brought to the Israelites an evil report of the land which they had scouted out..." (Numbers 13:32 KJV)

Evil means *"bad, inferior quality; wicked; a moral deficiency; inability to come up to good standards which will benefit. It is immoral activity against other people, whether by speech, by practice, or by offering improper sacrifices. This depicts a very negative inner attitude toward God or man."*

Their *wicked murmurings increased* and spread throughout the masses:

> *Then all the congregation lifted up their voices and cried, and the people wept that night.*
>
> *And all the sons of Israel grumbled against Moses and Aaron; and the whole congregation said to them,*
>
> *"Would that we had died in the land of Egypt! Or would that we had died in this wilderness!"* (Numbers 14:1-2 NASB)

The *evil, faithless words* of ten men infected thousands of people. Their *profane words* increased ungodliness within others to the point that a great judgment was wielded against them and the murmuring, grumbling congregation.

And the LORD spoke to Moses and Aaron, saying, "How long shall I bear with this evil congregation who are grumbling against Me? I have heard the complaints of the sons of Israel, which they are making against Me. Say to them, 'As I live,' says the LORD, 'just as you have spoken in My hearing, so I will surely do to you; your corpses shall fall in this wilderness, even all your numbered men, according to your complete number from twenty years old and upward, who have grumbled against Me.'" (Numbers 14:26-29 NASB)

As for the men whom Moses sent to spy out the land and who returned and made all the congregation grumble against him by bringing out a bad report concerning the land, even those men who brought out the very bad report of the land died by a plague before the LORD. (Numbers 14:36-37 NASB)

Where is our faith and confidence in God?

As I read the account of God's judgment, I was motivated to rethink my grumbling attitude. How about you? How much do we complain, moaning and groaning about this inconvenience or that difficulty? Do we perceive those *pebbles* in the road as though they were *towering mountains*? Where is our faith and confidence in God?

Josephus, a Jewish historian, described those ten spies as having elevated their words and perception about the land of Canaan *above* the word of God. They chose to place more value on their interpretation of the *promised land* than on God's view. They failed to remember that God's ways and thoughts were higher than theirs. His word was not settled as the authority in their lives. The ten spies' evil report defamed the LORD's power to deliver them!

Stop right here. Josephus' interpretation of those ten spies' response pierced through me like a spear. I began to wonder when I had ever placed my words higher than the word of the Lord. In II Corinthians 13:5 (NASB), Paul instructed us to: *"Test yourselves to see if you are in the faith; examine yourselves!"*

Personally, I was moved to repentance. Have you ever made statements like: *"You just wait and see. That store won't last a year;"* or *"You are such a scatterbrain. Why can't you remember what I told you?"* or *"Why should*

I try? I'll just fail. I can't do it," or *"Oh, forgive me, it's my memory; it's so bad."* Give Holy Spirit the freedom to convict you of sin and exhort you to a life of righteousness: a right relationship restored to God through the forgiveness of His Son and submission to Him.

> *If we say that we have no sin, we are deceiving ourselves, and the truth is not in us. If we confess our sins, He is faithful and righteous to forgive us our sins and to cleanse us from all unrighteousness.*
>
> (I John 1:8-9 NASB)

Allow this sobering word to remain with you for a long time. It will serve as a reminder to humble your words and thoughts to those of our Almighty God.

Life Application:

Every believer has God's Promised Land waiting for them to enter. Remember that Canaan represented one's inheritance gained through warfare. Consider this:

> *For though we walk in the flesh, we do not war according to the flesh, for the weapons of our warfare are not of the flesh, but divinely powerful for the destruction of fortresses. We are destroying speculations and every lofty thing raised up against the knowledge of God, and we are taking every thought captive to the obedience of Christ,*
>
> (II Corinthians 10:3-5 NASB)

We should not settle for anything less than God's best in our lives. We should embrace His truth rather than the defeating words of others or ourselves. Those destructive words and perceptions could cause us to *wander in the wilderness* instead of stepping into our inheritance, God's Promised Land. *Wilderness wanderings* represent failure to and unbelief in entering one's inheritance. When you are told: "Oh, that will never happen" or "that's impossible," or even, "there is no way for you to get that," don't accept it as true. Ask God what He thinks. Ask Him what His word declares about your hopes and dreams.

Where Must We Be Spiritually to Bless Others?

"For I know the plans I have for you," declares the LORD, "plans for welfare and not for calamity to give you a future and a hope."

(Jeremiah 29:11 NASB)

"A week, in the mountains, with snow."

Life Application:

My family and I have vacationed around the country for over thirty-five years. For several years, we used a timeshare exchange company to assist us. When our youngest son, David, was four, he announced that he wanted to go to the mountains for a week, wanting to see snow. We lived in Florida at that time, so SNOW was a big deal to him. David and I began to pray every night for: "a week, in the mountains, with snow."

Earlier that year, we had visited Blowing Rock, North Carolina, and loved it! So, we requested the same location for a week during Christmas. Our timeshare company offered no encouraging words; just the opposite: "There is no way you can get into that resort again, especially during Christmas." David and I continued to call upon God, asking for His favor. By the first week of December, we had not heard from our exchange company. Several phone calls later, covered with God's grace, we were given a week, during Christmas, in Blowing Rock. As we drove up the mountain, we could not see snow, but that meant the roads were clear and hazard-free. We continued to walk by faith and not by sight. We anticipated snow on Christmas Day. Much to our delight, HUGE snowflakes began to fall on Christmas morning! We caught it on camera. Blowing Rock became a *winter wonderland*. What a *faith builder* that was for David, and for me. God gave us the desires of our heart. He does not disappoint.

Over the years, David and I prayed for more *snow encounters*. Each time we prayed, God showed Himself creative and faithful. Whenever the snow occurred, the residents remarked how unusual it was! The sweetness of our Father God encouraged David and me. It has served as a memorial to the faithfulness of God to answer our prayers and to respond to our faith.

Examine where your faith is. Don't miss out on all the promises of God by listening to and accepting defeating words and circumstances. Bless yourself and others with the truth of God's word.

> *Take care, brethren, lest there should be in any one of you an evil, unbelieving heart, in falling away from the living God. But encourage one another day after day, as long as it is still called 'Today,' lest any one of you be hardened by the deceitfulness of sin. For we have become partakers of Christ, if we hold fast the beginning of our assurance firm until the end.* (Hebrews 3:12-14 NASB)

In speaking and declaring God's word of truth in the form of Spoken Blessings, we are warring against the spirits of deception, theft, and destruction. We recognize the enemy as one who comes to steal, kill, and destroy (John 10:10). We must hold fast to our confession, knowing that faith is required to enter God's promise (Hebrews 4:14; 11:6).

We can hear this message, but if it is not united by faith, it will not profit us.

> *"For good news came to us just as to them, but the message they heard did not benefit them, because they were not united by faith with those who listened."* (Hebrews 4:2 ESV)

When we hear the word of God's message and accept it for what it really is, the good news, then the word performs its work in us who believe.

> *This is why we continually thank God for your lives, because you received our message wholeheartedly. You embraced it not as the fabrication of men but as the word of God. And the word continues to be an energizing force in you who believe.* (I Thessalonians 2:13 TPT)

We are instructed to bless, which will pave the way for our inheriting our blessing, our land of milk and honey.

> *Never retaliate when someone treats you wrongly, nor insult those who insult you, but instead, respond by speaking a blessing over them—because a blessing is what God promised to give you.* (I Peter 3:9 TPT)

Consider what our lips can do for others:

The tongue of the righteous is as choice silver, ...
The lips of the righteous feed many, ...
The lips of the righteous bring forth what is acceptable, ...
(Proverbs 10:20,21,32 NASB)

Proverbs 10 identifies the positive potential of our mouths. James 3:5-12 exposes the opposite: the power of a sinful tongue. With our tongue, we can bless our Lord, but with it we curse men, who have been created in His image. If James 3 describes you, then, consider the cause.

"But the things that proceed out of the mouth come from the heart, and those defile the man." (Matthew 15:18 NASB)

When we love God with all our heart, there is no throne-room left for our pain and offense. How do you cleanse your heart of bad attitudes, doubt, fear, and unbelief?

Step 1: *Forgive those who have hurt you.* Ask God's Spirit to show you who you need to forgive. It is a choice you must make. It is a form of worship. When we love God with all our heart, there is no *throne-room* left for our pain and offense. Many have made idols out of their offenses. Forgive others, just as Christ has forgiven you.

"Be kind to one another, tenderhearted, forgiving one another, as God in Christ forgave you." (Ephesians 4:32 ESV)

The *Tallahassee Democrat* newspaper published an article by Julie Sevrens, entitled: "Forgiveness can heal." She identified that "scientists have launched research that has begun to demonstrate that forgiveness can positively enhance emotional and, quite possibly, physical health." Ms. Sevrens cited a study that linked anger with an increased risk of heart attacks and identified its negative influences on the body's immune system. Also noted was research which had found "that the less people forgave, the more diseases they had, and the more medical symptoms they reported." "You can actually change a person's well-being, their emotions, by helping them to forgive," stated Robert Enright, professor of educational psychology at the University of Wisconsin.[2]

Step 2: *Ask forgiveness from those you have hurt.* Ask God to forgive you for causing others pain. Hebrews 12:14 (NASB) clearly instructs us on this matter:

"Pursue peace with all men, and the sanctification without which no one will see the Lord."

Psalm 34:13-14 (NASB) admonishes us:

"Keep your tongue from evil, And your lips from speaking deceit. Depart from evil, and do good; Seek peace, and pursue it."

Step 3: *Speak death to the fruitless words you have spoken over your life and the lives of others.*

Freeda Bowers' *Give Me 40 Days* clearly explained and encouraged this step. It reminded me of my personal experience with the power of a *word curse* or *sowing a bad seed* into my life. I *sowed* that evil seed when I was in my early 20's.

Someone spoke cruel and offensive words to me concerning my appearance. My response to my pain was to speak a malediction or *word curse* over myself: I vowed that I would never give birth to a daughter. But, when our two boys were of preschool age, Cal and I were ready to ask God for a third child. Having two boys, I wanted a girl. As I prayed, God reminded me of my word curse; the evil seed I had sown. I was heartbroken. Could this mean that I would never have a daughter? I cried before the Lord with a broken and contrite heart, "Forgive me, Father, I didn't know what I was doing." God did not despise my repentance. In 1986, our beautiful princess, Elizabeth Ann, was born.

"Death and life are in the power of the tongue, And those who love it will eat its fruit." (Proverbs 18:21 NASB)

"The sacrifices of God are a broken spirit; a broken and contrite heart, O God, you will not despise." (Psalm 51:17 ESV)

---

2 (*Tallahassee Democrat*, "Forgiveness can heal," by Julie Sevrens, August 2, 1999)

Step 4: *Speak life over yourself and others, agreeing with the living word of God, trusting in the life-changing power of His Holy Spirit who lives within every believer in Jesus Christ.*

> *May you have faith like Abraham, as he believed that God would give him a child.*
>
> *May you call forth life over the barrenness of your body.*
>
> *May you agree with God's spoken word as He declared, 'Be fruitful and multiply.'*
>
> *May you call into being those children who do not yet exist, knowing that their spirits are in the presence of the Lord.*
>
> *May you have confidence that God knows each of your children before He places them within your womb.*
>
> *In Jesus' Name, Amen.* (Romans 4:17; Genesis 1:28; Jeremiah 1:5)

This is one of many types of blessings which speak *life* over someone. By faith, we can bless ourselves and others:

"By faith Isaac blessed Jacob and Esau, even regarding things to come. By faith Jacob, as he was dying, blessed each of the sons of Joseph, and worshiped, ..." (Hebrews 11:20,21 NASB)

As I referenced verse 21, I discovered Genesis 48:1-2, in which was described Israel's ailing condition: *"... your father is sick... Israel collected his strength and sat up in bed."* The meaning of "collected his strength" is *to make firm, to support, to prove courageous, valiant.* Often, it referred to a battle scene. Just think about that: a battle scene. There are and will be occasions in which we will experience a battle: to bless or to curse; to release a word of confidence in the power of God working within someone's life *or* to pronounce a condemning expectation of their personal abilities or inabilities. The battle is within. Jacob had to rely upon his inner strength because his physical body was weak and frail. We will have to do the same. Upon whose strength can we depend? The indwelling of the Spirit of Christ provides us with the support and resolve to speak *life*, not death, over others. Our spoken blessings will produce a lasting effect within the lives of others because our words carry the power of our eternal God. His word is settled in the heavens.

The Spoken Blessing I: A Spiritual Posture

"Standing firm in the heavens and fastened to eternity is the word of God." (Psalm 119:89 TPT)

Releasing a blessing over others provides an atmosphere of worship and a posture of reverence.

As our blessing focuses on God's faithful loving-kindness, the trustworthiness of His character, the abundance of His provision, and the never-failing forgiveness of the Cross, our hearts will move into awe and wonder of Him. Jacob moved from blessing his grandsons into worship of His God. We will do likewise.

Step 5: *Gain a new mindset; a new heart attitude by washing your mind and heart with the water of God's word.*

Many children grow up under, and I mean, *under*, the weight of a nickname. Parents begin calling a toddler some name, thinking it's cute or catchy: "Trouble," "Fireball," "Two-ton," "Klutzy," "Daredevil," etc. Some parents make excuses for a *tendency* within their child and verbalize it in the hearing of that child: "Oh, he's just a shy one," "Oh, I know he has a temper. It's that red hair, you know," "She doesn't like to read. I don't know what I'm going to do with her!" Older children may be burdened with names such as: "Computer Nerd," "Couch Potato," or "Geek." These nicknames may have different connotations within various groups of people, but rarely do they have an affirming or positive meaning.

Unfortunately, many children develop the characteristics that their parents emphasized by their nickname. If a person hears something often enough, they are likely to believe and embrace it. If a child gains attention for their *tendency*, they will work to maintain it to provide *more* attention for themselves.

Encouragement replaces condemnation.

Reading and believing, then speaking God's word as *truth*, will help remove the old ways of thinking about yourself and others. Truth replaces lies. Encouragement replaces condemnation. Bondage is destroyed; freedom is gained.

One historical figure who knew God's word and possessed a pure heart was Boaz. He chose to walk out his life in *faith*, *commitment*, and *expectancy*. In Chapter 3, we discussed Boaz's blessing of his workers who were reaping barley:

"May the LORD be with you."

His reapers responded:

"May the LORD bless you." (Ruth 2:4 NASB)

Boaz had confidence and *faith* in God's desire to be present within his life and in the lives of his workers. He was familiar with the Scriptures and *expected* God's blessing to rest upon him, his employees, and his fields. Boaz had a *commitment* to God's original plan and purpose of increase, fruitfulness and multiplication. Paul's analogy of a vessel of honor could be used to describe Boaz as one who was, *"useful to the Master, prepared for every good work."* (II Timothy 2:21 NASB)

What was the "good work" that I Peter 3:8-9 referred to: blessing others, and then, receiving our inherited blessing. Boaz not only knew *where* he needed to be, spiritually; he knew *where* God's blessings would flow. He had gained confidence in His God, by knowing His word:

> *Blessed shall you be in the city, and blessed shall you be in the country (field).*
>
> *Blessed shall be the ... produce of your ground... Blessed shall be your basket and your kneading bowl. Blessed shall you be when you come in, and blessed shall you be when you go out. The LORD will command the blessing upon you in your barns and in all that you put your hand to, and He will bless you in the land which the LORD your God gives you.* (Deuteronomy 28:3-6,8 NASB)

In Ruth 2:22-23 (NASB), a wise Naomi recognized *where* their blessing was and instructed Ruth:

> *And Naomi said to Ruth her daughter-in-law, 'It is good, my daughter, that you go out with his maids, lest others fall upon you in another field.' So she stayed close by the maids of Boaz in order to glean until the end of the barley harvest and the wheat harvest. And she lived with her mother-in-law.*

Ruth submitted to and obeyed the instruction of Naomi. *Barley* is a symbol of poverty, lowliness, and low reputation. Jesus taught in Matthew 5:3 (NASB): *"Blessed are the poor in spirit, for theirs is the kingdom of heaven."* We must recognize our impoverished, spiritual emptiness, allowing room for the King of Glory to enter our lives. Ruth had nothing, and she knew it. Her inheritance was linked to Naomi and to Boaz. She was no fool. Ruth understood the importance of staying close to her blessing. Take note that she stayed and gleaned through the wheat harvest. *Wheat* represents the *staff of life*, the *bread of Christ*, and of His saints.[3]

Jesus identified that the person with a humbled spirit, within which He is given control, is rewarded with His presence: the kingdom of heaven. Within His kingdom, all blessings flow.

Where are you spiritually?

1. Become confident in God's desire and eagerness to develop His divine nature within people.

God knows us as spiritual beings and gives us a physical body while we live on the earth. Therefore, He knew us before He placed us within our mother's womb (Jeremiah 1:5). Just as God had a plan for Jeremiah's life, He has a plan and purpose for you and me. As Jeremiah was to be consecrated and appointed as God's prophet, his character needed to reflect submission to God. Knowing that we all deal with sin, we need the redemptive power of Christ working within us, replacing our old ways with His new ways (II Corinthians 5:17). The working of His divine nature within us never ceases. God continually thinks about us: our past, our present, and our future (Jeremiah 29:11). As God consecrated Jeremiah, He sets us apart from the world to become pure and devoted to Him. This is the message of Paul's analogy of the vessels used for honor and dishonor (II Timothy 2:20).

In Psalm 139, David gave tribute to His Creator for his life:

For Thou didst form my inward parts; Thou didst weave me in my mother's womb.
I will give thanks to Thee, for I am fearfully and wonderfully made; wonderful are Thy works, and my soul knows it very well. My frame

---

[3] *Interpreting the Symbols and Types*, Kevin J. Conner, pp. 129,180

was not hidden from Thee, when I was made in secret, and skillfully wrought in the depths of the earth. Thine eyes have seen my unformed substance; and in Thy book there were all written, the days that were ordained for me, when as yet there was not one of them.

(Psalm 139:13-16 NASB)

Please read Psalm 139:17-18 provided by The Passion Translation:

Every single moment you are thinking of me!

How precious and wonderful to consider that you cherish me constantly in your every thought!

O God, your desires toward me are more than the grains of sand on every shore!

When I awake each morning, you're still with me.

Become confident that the Lord values each person and His image that is being developed within that person.

2. Choose to trust God to accomplish His divine plan for yourself and for others.

"For it is God who is at work in you, both to will and to work for His good pleasure." (Philippians 2:13 NASB)

The Greek word for *will* is *Thelo,* which means not only to will something, but also *pressing into action*. It refers to seeing one's desire to its execution: *"There is… a time for every purpose under the heaven."* *Energeo* is the Greek word for *work*. It refers to *being active and energetic, effective, proving oneself to be strong.*

Allow me to use these definitions to add depth to Philippians 2:13:

"For it is God who is actively working in you; pressing into action and energetically, effectively proving Himself strong in accomplishing His good desire and pleasure."

Definitions of words add richness and volume to our understanding of the message. Within us, we house thousands of definitions and concepts of words which may be accurate or erroneous. An example of this, is the word, *perfect.* Many people try to excuse their shortcomings by commenting: "Well, nobody's perfect." In saying this, the person admits to his flaws, trying to excuse his inability or his *unwillingness to sacrifice* to reach a higher standard. Thankfully, we serve and love a God who is strong when we are weak.

"For I am confident of this very thing, that He who began a good work in you will perfect it until the day of Christ Jesus." (Philippians 1:6 NASB)

In other words, God will finish, complete, and accomplish what He started. He is not a quitter. He is our beginning and our end.

"Therefore you are to be perfect, as your heavenly Father is perfect."
(Matthew 5:48 NASB)

"And let endurance have its perfect result, that you may be perfect and complete, lacking in nothing." (James 1:4 NASB)

The Greek word being used in the latter two passages refers to *completed growth*. Yet, it is not a static state. This level of perfection describes one who has attained his moral end, the goal for which he was intended: *to be obedient in Christ*. Having reached this level, new opportunities will be opened before him to have Christ formed in him more and more.

Please read James 1:4 in The Passion Translation:

And then as your endurance grows even stronger it will release perfection into every part of your being until there is nothing missing and nothing lacking.

And all of us, as with unveiled face, [because we] continued to behold [in the Word of God] as in a mirror the glory of the Lord, are constantly being transfigured into His very own image in ever increasing splendor and from one degree of glory to another; [for this comes] from the Lord [Who is] the Spirit." (II Corinthians 3:18 AMP)

Thus, we recognize the magnitude of God's work within us and others. It gives Him great delight and pleasure to accomplish His plan in our lives. As proud parents, Cal and I have watched our children walk down the aisles of their high school and college graduations; tassels swinging, faces beaming, and hands waving with "Pomp and Circumstance" playing loudly. We have participated in the continual, energetic work that a parent contributes to a child's education and training. As parents, we have had to prove ourselves strong on behalf of our children's sake. Besides the Lord, parents should be their child's strongest advocate, defending them and correcting them, helping them to achieve their destiny in God's Kingdom. Yet, we are just a shadow of the perfect work that God delights in accomplishing within His children.

3. Approach your relationship with God and your life with: *expectancy*, *faith*, **and** *commitment*.

As we discussed in Chapter 1, these three components were obvious within the parents who brought their children to Jesus. Review their story in Mark 10:13-16 (NASB):

And they were bringing children to Him so that He might touch them; and the disciples rebuked them. But when Jesus saw this, He was indignant and said to them, 'Permit the children to come to Me; do not hinder them; for the kingdom of God belongs to such as these. Truly I say to you, whoever does not receive the kingdom of God like a child shall not enter it at all.' And He took them in His arms and began blessing them, laying His hands upon them.

The blessing of the Lord sets us apart...

Notice the perseverance of the parents. They did not allow the disciples to stop them from reaching Jesus. We should always seek after God; always desiring to be in His presence. Our firsthand, personal experience with Jesus should be so fulfilling that we are motivated to be with Him. The parents in this passage had either heard about or had firsthand experience with the power and authority of Christ. They had *expectations* and *faith* in Jesus to do something good for their children. We are no different. We want our children to receive the fullest measure of blessings possible. A parent wants their child's needs and wants to be met.

The parents in Mark 10 were *committed* to the *task at hand*. "*To everything there is a season, and a time to every purpose under the heaven*" (Ecclesiastes 3:1 KJV). They wanted the blessing of the Lord to rest upon their children. Should we desire any less for our children and for others?

When Jesus took their children into His strong arms, He blessed them, consecrating them for divine use. He set them apart from the mundane and profane things of this world. The blessing of the Lord sets us apart, sets our future apart, and sets our eternal destiny apart for His glory and for the multiplication of His Kingdom. In a similar fashion, Jesus blessed the five loaves and two fish. The food was miraculously multiplied for the feeding of thousands and for bringing glory to His heavenly Father (Mark 6:41). When we bless others, miraculous events occur, needs are met, lives are restored, hope is encouraged, truth is imparted, all to the glory of God.

The children's parents knew *where* they could find and receive their blessing. *Where* is your blessing? Under whose authority, under whose covering should you submit?

***Where* can you give blessings to others?**

Ask God to provide you with divine appointments every day. Ask Him to help you identify them and to be in tune with His Spirit, so that you may give a blessing in the proper season and at the right time.

Life Application:

One Saturday evening, I ran into a store to purchase something. As I was checking out, the clerk sighed deeply, expressing how tired she was. Despondently, she mentioned her being scheduled to work on Sunday, not being able to attend her church service. I encouraged her to invite Jesus to work with her the next day. Then, I spoke a blessing of God's rest and restoration over her. The clerk's countenance changed. She became more cheerful and relaxed.

***Where* must we be, spiritually, to bless others? How should our "horizontal" {↔} relationships appear?**

1. harmonious
2. sympathetic
3. brotherly

4. kind-hearted
   5. humble in spirit

We must love our neighbor as ourselves (Matthew 22:39).

What must happen within our hearts and minds to enable us to bless?

   1. cleanse ourselves from worldly, empty chatter and wickedness
   2. forgive others and seek forgiveness from others
   3. speak death to bad words and attitudes
   4. speak life, agreeing with God's word of faith

What truths from God's word must be grounded within our being?

- God desires for us to become vessels of honor: our speech should feed many and speak forth what is acceptable.
- God desires to bless us and others.
- God has a purpose for every person.
- God is trustworthy and will accomplish His will and His work.

***Where* must we be in our "vertical" {↕} relationship with God?**

His Spirit of truth must have complete authority in our heart, soul, and mind. When combined, our "horizontal" and "vertical" relationships portray the Cross {†}, through which our inherited blessing originates and emanates.

What mindsets and conditions of our hearts must prevail to allow us the freedom to bless and not curse?

   1. We should be full of *faith* in Jesus.
   2. We should have *expectancy* in our hearts.
   3. We should be *committed* to His goals and purposes.

His goal is for you to walk in His blessing:

> *May the Lord cause you to prosper and excel in all that you do.*
> *May all that you do be done to the glory of God.*
> *May others see your good work and offer praise to Him and Him alone.*

May you be perfected in your obedience to Him.

May you be reassured that He loves you and takes great delight in spending time with you.

May you reserve special sessions of 'one-on-one' time with the Lord.

May He share with you His special intimacies, preserved for His righteous ones.

May you offer a sacrifice of praise and thanksgiving for the wonderful gift of His love.

In Jesus' Name, Amen.

Journal of My Journey with the Spoken Blessing

At this time, I would describe my relationship with God as:

_____
_____
_____

I will improve it by:

_____
_____
_____

I will forgive:

_____
_____
_____

I will ask forgiveness for:

_____
_____
_____

The Spoken Blessing I: A Spiritual Posture

I will improve my relationships with others by:

_____
_____
_____

Write a blessing for a family member or friend.

_____
_____
_____
_____

"He who loves purity of heart and whose speech is gracious, the king is his friend." (Proverbs 22:11 NASB)

Chapter Five

Why Should We Use the Spoken Blessing?

> *Then the LORD spoke to Moses, saying, "Speak to Aaron and to his sons, saying,*
> *'Thus you shall bless the sons of Israel. You shall say to them:*
> *The LORD bless you, and keep you;*
> *the LORD make His face shine on you, and be gracious to you;*
> *the LORD lift up His countenance on you, and give you peace.'*
> *" So they shall invoke My name on the sons of Israel, and I then will bless them."* (Numbers 6:22-27 NASB)

To *invoke* means to *bless*, to *call for a blessing*, to *put into use* or to *call forth*.

The King James translation reads: *"And they shall put My name upon the children of Israel, and I will bless them."*

God's name reflects His character, His person. Is there anything more powerful than His name? We are *to use* and *call forth* His name. Who is like the Lord? Is there anything more perfect than His divine name, His holy nature?

The Spoken Blessing I: A Spiritual Posture

Recall that God has shown Himself to be committed to:

1. His creation
2. His covenant
3. His name and character.

Who was instructed to *invoke* or *put God's name upon* the people?

Aaron and his sons were given the command. Who were they? Aaron and his sons had been appointed and anointed as the Lord's priests. God gave them and their positions certain authority, responsibilities and privileges. These priests understood the gravity and consequences of their office.

As Aaron and his sons were the priests within the Old Covenant, who are their counterparts within the New Covenant, in this present dispensation of Christ's Church?

> *You also, as living stones, are being built up as a spiritual house for a holy priesthood, to offer up spiritual sacrifices acceptable to God through Jesus Christ. But you are a CHOSEN RACE, A ROYAL PRIESTHOOD, A HOLY NATION, A PEOPLE FOR GOD'S OWN POSSESSION, that you may proclaim the excellencies of Him who has called you out of darkness into His marvelous light;"* (I Peter 2:5,9 NASB)

"But you will be called the priests of the LORD; you will be spoken of as ministers of our God. You will eat the wealth of nations, and in their riches you will boast." (Isaiah 61:6 NASB)

You and I, believers in the Lord Jesus Christ, are His *royal priesthood*. As we serve as priests to God, we execute His instruction and command to bless.

Why should we use *the Spoken Blessing*? We are to proclaim the excellencies of our Lord, and we are directed to do so.

Recall I Peter 3:9 (NASB): *"...but giving a blessing instead; for you were called for the very purpose that you might inherit a blessing."*

In Greek, the word *called* is *kaleo* which means to *invite*; of the *divine invitation to participate in the blessings of redemption*; to *be called by name*. It suggests either *vocation* or *destination*.

> *We are to look for and anticipate God providing opportunities for us to bless others.*

As we serve God as priests and ministers, we are to fulfill His will and His commitment to *bless*. As we bless, we receive blessings as Galatians 6:7-10 (NASB) identifies:

> *Do not be deceived, God is not mocked: for whatever a man sows, this he will also reap. For the one who sows to his own flesh shall from the flesh reap corruption, but the one who sows to the Spirit shall from the Spirit reap eternal life. And let us not lose heart in doing good, for in due time we shall reap if we do not grow weary. So then, while we have opportunity, let us do good to all men, and especially to those who are of the household of the faith.*

We are to look for and anticipate God providing opportunities for us to bless others.

Ask Him what you can do each day that would bring Him glory and honor. Anticipation of God going before us creates an excitement and a joy that is visible upon our countenance, heard within our words and witnessed in the spiritual realm.

> *You are the light of the world. A city set on a hill cannot be hidden. Nor do men light a lamp, and put it under the peck-measure, but on the lampstand; and it gives light to all who are in the house. Let your light shine before men in such a way that they may see your good works, and glorify your Father who is in heaven.*
>
> (Matthew 5:14-16 NASB)

> *Obedience in this area has a direct consequence: inheriting our blessing.*

Remember, we are being built up (and we are building up others) as a spiritual house through which we offer to God spiritual sacrifices. We give His light to those who are in our dwelling or workplace, within our sphere of influence. Each of us has a realm in which we work, live, serve and recreate. What impact are we having in these areas? Do others know that we are believers in the Lord Jesus?

Within these different spheres, throughout our *walks of life,* we will experience offenses, maledictions, biases and misunderstandings. Our command is to bless and to not return the curse. How many of us can attest to the *sacrifice of our flesh* when we *do not* retaliate with harsh words or criticism? How many of us have poured *cool* words on the top of *hot heads?* We must continue to encourage and help each other achieve this level of humility and submission to His command because obedience in this area has a direct consequence: inheriting our blessing (I Peter 3:9). Not returning evil for evil, but giving a blessing instead, is an *overcomer's outlook.* Overcomers receive their inheritance (Revelation 21:7).

Consider a biblical character who satisfied his physical desires or served his *flesh,* disregarding the value of his spiritual inheritance:

> *See to it that no one comes short of the grace of God; that no root of bitterness springing up causes trouble, and by it many be defiled; that there be no immoral or godless person like Esau, who sold his own birthright for a single meal. For you know that even afterwards, when he desired to inherit a blessing, he was rejected, for he found no place for repentance, though he sought for it with tears.*
>
> (Hebrews 12:15-17 NASB)

Life Application:

When someone offends us, we have a choice to make: to bless or to curse them. A blessing operates within the spiritual realm of ourselves and the offender. A curse patronizes the fleshly, carnal level of both people. *We must decide into which realm we will sow; for, from that realm, we will reap.* If we place more value in retaliation and protecting our image, reputation or *rights,* then, we place less value on our future spiritual inheritance. There will be no repentance found within our hearts. We will continue throughout life with a bitter, unchanged heart. We will lose the promised blessing, though we seek it with tears.

Why Should We Use the Spoken Blessing?

A side note: Esau loved his *flesh* and wanted to have immediate gratification instead of sacrificing and patiently waiting for his promised inheritance and blessing. Let this be a warning to us! Spend time with this Life Application. Meditate on it until God's Spirit completes His instruction for you. Allow Him to personalize this lesson.

Chuck D. Pierce, a man who serves as a mighty intercessor of God, sent a word from the Lord directing believers to "Seven Days of Stillness: A Prayer Focus to Renew Your Spirit." This directive was dated August 31, 2004. The Lord instructed us to be still and allow Him to quiet and purify our hearts. Our sin had to be dealt a fatal blow. Our hearts had to be purified. The message that pierced my heart was that I had to eliminate all "dangerous emotions" that would cause me to miss the fullest measure and benefits of Jesus' Salvation.

The word of the Lord said:

> *My people are filled with dangerous emotions. I want to settle their emotions so that their mind will think the same way that I think. Unless they allow Me to deal with their dangerous emotions they will miss many blessings that I have for the future. Many will end up striking the rock as Moses did out of a dangerous emotion instead of speaking to the rock and miss their door of entry for this season. Tell My people to be still.*
>
> *I am calling for a Jericho stillness. This warfare call is important for the future of My people. If they will come before Me for seven straight days and allow Me to still their hearts and quiet their spirits, that which has been invincible in their past and has kept them from moving into their future will fall before them. Tell MY people to still their hearts before Me.*

I observed this Stillness Fast in 2004. I have chosen to follow a similar fast since then. God was faithful to show me what I had to accomplish, every day, to overcome my dangerous emotion. Esau's love of self was more important to him than his inheritance in God (Genesis 25:29-34). Moses' self-love overshadowed his love for the Lord and His Promised Land (Numbers 20:1-13). I do not want to love myself, my emotions, my rights or reputation more than I love God and His Christ. I deeply desire for His Kingdom to come and His will to be done in my life while I live on this earth.

The Spoken Blessing I: A Spiritual Posture

May you reach the point in your life where you can declare as Paul did:

> *But I do not consider my life of any account as dear to myself, in order that I may finish my course, and the ministry which I received from the Lord Jesus, to testify solemnly of the gospel of the grace of God." "For I did not shrink from declaring to you the whole purpose of God.* (Acts 20:24,27 NASB)

May you follow Paul's example found in Acts 20:32,35 (NASB):

> *And now I commend you to God and to the word of His grace, which is able to build you up and to give you the inheritance among all those who are sanctified." "In everything I showed you that by working hard in this manner you must help the weak and remember the words of the Lord Jesus, that He Himself said, 'It is more blessed to give than to receive.'*

Makarios is the Greek word used in verse 35, which is translated as *blessed*. It indicates the state of the believer in Christ. The believer is indwelt by God because of Christ and as a result is fully satisfied. A *blessed* person is one whom *God makes fully satisfied*, not because of favorable circumstances, but because *He indwells the believer through Christ*. To be *makarios, blessed,* is equivalent to having God's kingdom within one's heart. Submission to the control and authority of God's Holy Spirit allows us to experience the kingdom of God in our lives.

When we bless others, we speak well of them, we consecrate them for divine use, we call forth God's name and character to be formed within them through the presence and power of His Spirit. As we speak a blessing over someone's life, we build them up, encouraging them to operate in the spiritual realm and to focus on their destiny within God's Kingdom. A result of speaking blessings is to assist others in turning away from their iniquities (Acts 3:26).

As Paul recognized the ministry which he had been given (Acts 20:24), you and I have been given the ministry of reconciliation as stated in II Corinthians 5:18-20 (NASB):

> *Now all these things are from God, who reconciled us to Himself through Christ, and gave us the ministry of reconciliation, namely, that God was in Christ reconciling the world to Himself, not*

Why Should We Use the Spoken Blessing?

> *counting their trespasses against them, and He has committed to us the word of reconciliation. Therefore, we are ambassadors for Christ, as though God were entreating through us; we beg you on behalf of Christ, be reconciled to God.*

God so deeply longed for His people to be *one with Him* that Jesus humbled Himself to suffer death on a cross, before the foundations of the earth had been laid (1 Peter 1:18-20). God is All-knowing. He knew what it would take for His creation to be restored and redeemed from sin. God desired for His creation to be reconciled to Him and restored to his original position of *authority*, his original covering of His *glory*, his original *fellowship* with Him. God gave Adam and Eve authority:

> *And God blessed them and said to them, Be fruitful, multiply; and fill the earth, and subdue it [using all its vast resources in the service of God and man]; and have dominion over the fish of the sea, the birds of the air, and over every living creature that moves upon the earth.* (Genesis 1:28 AMP)

Originally, God's spiritual image was the composition of Adam and Eve:

"Then God said, 'Let Us make man in Our image, according to Our likeness.'" (Genesis 1:26 NASB)

"And the man and his wife were both naked and were not embarrassed or ashamed in each other's presence." (Genesis 2:25 AMP)

We also read about this manifestation of God's *glory* in Exodus 34:29. Moses' *face shown* as a result of being in the presence of God. *Shone* refers to *rays* emanating from Moses' face. That external manifestation faded (II Corinthians 3:7). But the ministry of the Spirit transforms us from glory to glory, restoring within us the original image of God, His nature and character.

> *We can all draw close to him with the veil removed from our faces. And with no veil we all become like mirrors who brightly reflect the glory of the Lord Jesus. We are being transfigured into his very image as we move from one brighter level of glory to another. And this glorious transfiguration comes from the Lord, who is the Spirit.*
> (II Corinthians 3:18 TPT)

The Spoken Blessing I: A Spiritual Posture

Adam and Eve, originally, experienced intimate *fellowship* with God as is implied:

> *And they heard the sound of the LORD God walking in the garden in the cool of the day, and the man and his wife hid themselves from the presence of the LORD God among the trees of the garden. Then the LORD God called to the man, and said to him, "Where are you?"* (Genesis 3:8,9 NASB)

As ministers of reconciliation, we can bless others with the word of God, building them up in their faith, encouraging restoration of their authority, God's glory, and fellowship with Him (II Corinthians 10:8). We can declare with confidence:

> *May God cause you to prosper and excel in all that you do as He did Joseph.*
>
> *May others elevate you into positions of authority as they regard God's favor upon you.*
>
> *May others be blessed through your relationship with the Lord.*
> (Genesis 39:2-6)
>
> *May the Lord be your glory and the One who lifts your head.*
>
> *May you trust in God to complete and perfect the good work He has begun in you.*
>
> *May you be trained in His righteousness, moving from glory to glory.*
>
> *May you be conformed to the image of His Son, who is full of glory.* (Psalm 3:3; Philippians 1:6; Romans 8:29; 9:23)
>
> *May God make known to you the path of life.*
>
> *May you discover that in His presence is fullness of joy; in His right hand there are pleasures forever.*
>
> *May you know Christ, the power of His resurrection and the fellowship of His sufferings, being conformed to His death to attain to the resurrection from the dead.*
>
> *May you enter into eternal fellowship with your Lord.* (Psalm 16:11; Philippians 3:10-11)

Why Should We Use the Spoken Blessing?

As fellow believers we can exhibit similar support as Aaron and Hur did for Moses during the Israelites' battle against the Amalekites. Aaron and Hur stood with Moses on the top of a hill, as they observed the battle. Moses had agreed to hold the rod of God in his hand for the duration of the battle.

"And Moses said unto Joshua, Choose us out men, and go out, fight with Amalek: tomorrow I will stand on the top of the hill with the rod of God in mine hand." (Exodus 17:9 KJV)

Metteh is the Hebrew word used for *rod*. It can reference a branch, a tribe, a rod for chastening or correcting, a scepter for ruling, a lance to be thrown, a walking staff for a support of life.[4]

The battle was noticeably affected by Moses' position or posture with this rod.

"So it came about when Moses held his hand up, that Israel prevailed, and when he let his hand down, Amalek prevailed." (Exodus 17:11 NASB)

Aaron and Hur made the association of victory and defeat as it related to Moses' posture with the rod. They decided to do something.

"Do not withhold good from those to whom it is due, when it is in your power to do it." (Proverbs 3:27 NASB)

> *But Moses' hands were heavy. Then they took a stone and put it under him, and he sat on it; and Aaron and Hur supported his hands, one on one side and one on the other. Thus his hands were steady until the sun set.* (Exodus 17:12 NASB)

Picture this: *Aaron, a mountain of strength or an enlightened one,* stood on one side of his younger brother, while *Hur, noble or splendor,* stood on the opposite side of Moses. Tradition has it that Hur was the husband of Miriam, the older sister of Aaron and Moses.[5]

> *Behold, how good and pleasant it is when brothers dwell in unity! It is like the precious oil on the head, running down on the beard, on the beard of Aaron, running down on the collar of his robes!*

---

4   *e-Sword X the Sword of the LORD with an electronic edge,* Rick Meyers, 9.5 version, 2025
5   *All the Men of the Bible,* Herbert Lockyer, pp. 19,151

The Spoken Blessing I: A Spiritual Posture

*It is like the dew of Hermon, which falls on the mountains of Zion!
For there the LORD has commanded the blessing, life forevermore.*
(Proverbs 133:1-3 ESV)

The union of the brethren steadied the hands of Moses. They were united in their effort.

Steady is the English translation for *emuwnah* which means *firmness, steadfastness; faithfulness, trust, honesty.* It is derived from the word: *aman*, from which we get our word: *amen*. Aaron and Hur came alongside of Moses to assist him in maintaining his posture as he held up the *ruling, chastening authority of God*. Consider the effect of their help:

"So Joshua overwhelmed Amalek and his people with the edge of the sword." (Exodus 17:13 NASB)

Why should we use *the Spoken Blessing*?

Even if our hands are empty, our hearts are not.

Life Application:

Our fellow believers, even spiritual leaders, need physical and spiritual strength. Life is hard and the going gets tough. We can offer each other support. Many times, needs are obvious. Someone's countenance, or posture and the words they speak serve as a clear signal for us to do something! Even if our hands are empty, our hearts are not. We have the River of Life flowing through us and overflowing from us for the benefit of others. God's life-giving word can be spoken to refresh weary bones and uplift sagging spirits.

Why should we use *the Spoken Blessing*? It can change the results of a battle, even, the atmosphere and strength of a city:

"By the blessing of the upright a city is exalted, but by the mouth of the wicked it is torn down." (Proverbs 11:11 NASB)

Spoken Blessings can change someone's future.

Several years ago, I spoke to a women's group. I addressed the issue of using nicknames for our children and how detrimental some could be. At the close of my presentation, a mother of twin girls confided that one of her two-year-olds was very clumsy, and, in fact, she had been calling her that: "Clumsy." She was moved to repentance and change. No longer would this little girl grow up under such a burden but would be strengthened and encouraged by her mother's blessings. I rejoiced for the lives that were changed.

Consider the power of your words. Recall the truth revealed in Proverbs 18:21 (NASB): *"Death and life are in the power of the tongue, and those who love it will eat its fruit."*

That two-year-old daughter would no longer have destructive words spoken against her. Robert S. McGee explained in his book, *Father Hunger*: "No other human bond is as strong as the one between parent and child." As parents, we must not underestimate the power of our affection, attention and our words. Mr. McGee identified that "a major element of their (father and mother) parental duties was to pass along God's love to their growing children." "Of all the influences we will ever encounter---environment, personality, role models, peers, or whatever---nothing usually affects us as strongly as our parents. People can be brought up in harsh environments, experience severe poverty, run around with peers who drink or do drugs, yet overcome all these obstacles and go on to achieve great things. In almost every such case, these people attribute their success to parents who truly cared."

Over the years, I have sat in various waiting rooms and thumbed through magazines. Different stories have caught my attention. One such story tore at my heart. An adult male earnestly tried to reach his dying father's bedside. But he was minutes too late. He collapsed beside his father's lifeless body, weeping, uncontrollably. Minutes later, he looked into his father's face and begged: "Please, Daddy, just tell me that you love me. Just tell me that you're proud of me. I love you, Daddy. Please, just say something." *Father Hunger* highlighted: "In the hearts of many men and women is a hollow place. We long for the blessing that only a father can give. Great numbers of adults continually struggle through life with unresolved emotional problems that can be traced back to the lack of a father's love. The emotional emptiness produced by father hunger can be destructive, powerful and long lasting. We all thrive on the love-signals we receive from our parents."

Even if you see your children acting in a clumsy, forgetful, or careless way, time and time again, don't start calling them names; don't begin projecting a negative expectation about their abilities. Exchange your frustration for a focus on what God wants them to become: graceful (or full of His grace), exercising a good memory, attentive and alert to the consequences of their actions. The Scriptures are full of examples of God's restoration for our lives:

Restoration honors God.

The Spirit of the Lord GOD is upon me, because the LORD has anointed me to bring good news to the afflicted; He has sent me to bind up the brokenhearted, to proclaim liberty to captives, and freedom to prisoners; to proclaim the favorable year of the LORD, and the day of vengeance of our God; to comfort all who mourn, to grant those who mourn in Zion, giving them a garland instead of ashes, the oil of gladness instead of mourning, the mantle of praise instead of a spirit of fainting. So they will be called oaks of righteousness, the planting of the LORD, that He may be glorified." (Isaiah 61:1-3 NASB)

Restoration honors God. When His people are blessed, others notice, just as Potiphar took note of God's blessing Joseph. God's people bless Him, also. Our son, whom I described in the Preface, was headed down a rocky road. Using *the Spoken Blessing*, our attention was redirected to what God wanted to accomplish in his life. During Peyton's teenage years, different guest speakers at our church prophesied over him: "World-changer." As I write this, Peyton has worked for eighteen years as a Physician's Assistant within the Emergency Room of Tallahassee's largest hospital. He has credited God with equipping him with insight and discernment to recognize underlying causes for patients' illnesses. Peyton has recognized the power and value of God's faithfully working within his life. God has coupled Peyton's compassionate heart with this vocation. A love for science has been exponentially multiplied and used. Peyton is on track with his destiny... all to the glory of God.

Why should we use the Spoken Blessing?

It is a spiritual posture of confidence in God.

It is an expression of our faith and a spiritual posture of confidence in God.

Jesus taught His disciples about the expression of one's faith, the continual results that faith should produce and the importance of forgiveness.

> *And on the next day, when they had departed from Bethany, He became hungry. And seeing at a distance a fig tree in leaf, He went to see if perhaps He would find anything on it; and when He came to it, He found nothing but leaves, for it was not the season for figs. And He answered and said to it, "May no one ever eat fruit from you again!" And His disciples were listening.*
>
> *And as they were passing by in the morning, they saw the fig tree withered from the roots up. And being reminded, Peter said to Him, 'Rabbi, behold, the fig tree which You cursed has withered.' And Jesus answered saying to them, 'Have faith in God. Truly I say to you, whoever says to this mountain, "Be taken up and cast into the sea," and does not doubt in his heart, but believes that what he says is going to happen, it shall be granted him. Therefore I say to you, all things for which you pray and ask, believe that you have received them, and they shall be granted you. And whenever you stand praying, forgive, if you have anything against anyone; so that your Father also who is in heaven may forgive you your transgressions.*
> (Mark 11:12-14, 20-25 NASB)

Jesus had a need: He was hungry. Every day you will encounter people with needs: they are hungry for the Lord's presence in their lives. The leaves on this fig tree indicated that it was alive: the leaf is a symbol of life amidst prosperity or adversity. Many, many Christians, or *churchgoers* are alive, but don't bear fruit for the benefit of others. They may attend church because it is the *socially acceptable* thing to do or to have their personal needs met, but rarely do they assist or serve others. Their hearts are not seeking a submitted, intimate relationship with the Lord. Their focus is on themselves and not Him. *Woe* to those who call themselves *Christians*, but do not bear fruit for the Kingdom.

Wow to those who place their total trust and confidence in the Lord!

> *Blessed is the man who trusts in the LORD And whose trust is the LORD.*
>
> *For he will be like a tree planted by the water; that extends its roots by a stream and will not fear when the heat comes; but its leaves will be green, and it will not be anxious in a year of drought nor cease to yield fruit.* (Jeremiah 17:7-8 NASB)

We are to yield fruit regardless of the external conditions. Why are we able to do that? How is it that heat and drought would not cause our fruit to cease?

Because our waters come from out of the sanctuary.

> *And on the banks of the river on both its sides, there shall grow all kinds of trees for food; their leaf shall not fade nor shall their fruit fail [to meet the demand]. Each tree shall bring forth new fruit every month, [these supernatural qualities being] because their waters came from out of the sanctuary. And their fruit shall be for food and their leaves for healing.* (Ezekiel 47:12 AMP)

Why are we able to continually bear fruit? Our water, our sustenance comes from the sanctuary, the holy place. Who is our holy place?

> *Now on the final and most important day of the Feast, Jesus stood, and He cried in a loud voice, If any man is thirsty, let him come to Me and drink! He who believes in Me [who cleaves to and trusts in and relies on Me] as the Scripture has said, From his innermost being shall flow [continuously] springs and rivers of living water.*
> (John 7:37, 38 AMP)

We are the temple of the living God (II Corinthians 6:16). The life of Jesus, His Spirit, flows through us and continually produces fruit for the feeding and restoration of the people.

In II Timothy 4:2 (NASB), this analogy is continued: *"Preach the word; be ready in season and out of season; reprove, rebuke, exhort, with great patience and instruction."*

We are to proclaim Christ's victory to the downcast and fallen ones which is the act of Christ. There is an urgency in the phrase: "be ready." We are to continually bear fruit for the nurturing and renewal of others. As we serve others, we serve the Lord Jesus. Jesus was hungry and looking for fruit. Will He find fruit on our fig tree?

In Chapter 4, we discussed the importance of forgiveness. Jesus clearly addressed this need. Acting in the likeness of Christ, we forgive. Then *we* will be forgiven. There is an urgency in being ready to forgive. Forgiveness feels so good. My heart always feels much cleaner, purer, when I have forgiven someone, or have asked for forgiveness. The enemy cannot bring words of condemnation against me. Doubt, fear and unbelief have no place within me. My spiritual posture is strong in the Lord. I can speak to those mountains, and they will move. I can minister to others with authority, sharing God's glory, encouraging their intimate fellowship with the Lord as I speak blessings over them.

My spiritual posture is strong in the Lord.

By faith, you and I can call into being that which does not exist within a person's life:

> *For this reason it is by faith, that it might be in accordance with grace, in order that the promise may be certain to all the descendants, not only to those who are of the Law, but also to those who are of the faith of Abraham, who is the father of us all, (as it is written, "A FATHER OF MANY NATIONS HAVE I MADE YOU") in the sight of Him whom he believed, even God, who gives life to the dead and calls into being that which does not exist. In hope against hope he believed, in order that he might become, a father of many nations, according to that which had been spoken, "SO SHALL YOUR DESCENDANTS BE."* (Romans 4:16-18 NASB)

To believe is to become.

Another Old Testament figure exercised his faith and confidence in God. He trusted God's Almighty power to give life to the dead, calling into being that which did not exist.

> *The hand of the LORD was upon me, and He brought me out by the Spirit of the LORD and set me down in the middle of the valley; and it was full of bones. And He caused me to pass among them round about, and behold, there were very many on the surface of the valley; and lo, they were very dry. And He said to me, "Son of man, can these bones live?" And I answered, "O Lord GOD, Thou knowest." Again He said to me, "Prophesy over these bones, and say to them, 'O dry bones, hear the word of the LORD.' Thus says the Lord GOD to these bones, 'Behold, I will cause breath to enter you that you may come to life. And I will put sinews on you, make flesh grow back on you, cover you with skin, and put breath in you that you may come alive; and you will know that I am the LORD.'*
>
> *So I prophesied as I was commanded; and as I prophesied, there was a noise, and behold, a rattling; and the bones came together, bone to its bone. And I looked, and behold, sinews were on them, and flesh grew, and skin covered them; but there was no breath in them. Then He said to me, "Prophesy to the breath, prophesy, son of man, and say to the breath, 'Thus says the Lord GOD, "Come from the four winds,*
>
> *O breath, and breathe on these slain, that they come to life."" So I prophesied as He commanded me, and the breath came into them, and they came to life, and stood on their feet, an exceedingly great army.* (Ezekiel 37:1-10 NASB)

When you entwine your obedience and faith with the power of God's Holy Spirit, an exceedingly great army will arise to their feet.

We encounter people whose hope has dried up, whose dreams are withered, whose zest for life is all but gone. They truly need resurrection power working in their lives.

Jesus is the Resurrection.

And Who is Jesus? He is the Word.

> *In the beginning was the Word, and the Word was with God, and the Word was God....And the Word became flesh, and dwelt among us, and we beheld His glory, glory as of the only begotten from the Father, full of grace and truth.* (John 1:1,14 NASB)

> *Ezekiel had to speak; he had to give "voice" to the word of the Lord.*

Ezekiel *beheld* the *glory of the living God* as he watched those bones flying across the sky, being assembled into human structures. He *beheld* the *glory of creation* as God formed sinew, flesh and skin to cover those dry bones. This obedient prophet *witnessed* the *resurrection power* as the breath of life entered those bodies, causing color to flow, strength to surge and keen alertness to quicken them. Ezekiel was surrounded by the activity of the Holy Trinity. What an awesome reward for faith, spoken faith, and obedience. Ezekiel had to speak; he had to give "voice" to the word of the LORD.

When God hears you speaking His words of truth and life over someone, He honors His word and the faith you are exercising:

"Then the LORD said to me, 'You have seen well, for I am watching over My word to perform it.'" (Jeremiah 1:12 NASB)

God released a similar message through the prophet Isaiah: *"So shall My word be which goes forth from My mouth; It shall not return to Me empty, Without accomplishing what I desire, And without succeeding in the matter for which I sent it."* (Isaiah 55:11 NASB)

From the beginning, the power of God's spoken word has been recognizable: *"Then God said, 'Let there be light;' and there was light."*
(Genesis 1:3 NASB)

God's spoken word has power to create life and light within a person, a city, a nation. God has given us the *freedom to choose what we will speak and confess* over ourselves, over others and over our surroundings. Joshua, the leader of God's people, emphatically announced: *"... choose for yourselves today whom you will serve: ... but as for me and my house, we will serve the LORD."* (Joshua 24:15 NASB)

Why should we use the Spoken Blessing?

1. We are commanded to bless others.

"But I say to you who hear, love your enemies, do good to those who hate you, bless those who curse you, pray for those who mistreat you."

(Luke 6:27-28 NASB)

2. We are to serve the Lord all our days.

"... Truly I say to you, to the extent that you did it to one of these brothers of Mine, even the least of them, you did it to Me."

(Matthew 25:40 NASB)

3. We have been given the ministry of reconciliation.

"For we are fellow workmen [joint promoters, laborers together] with and for God; you are God's garden and vineyard and field under cultivation, [you are] God's building." (I Corinthians 3:9 AMP)

4. We can affect many lives for the Kingdom of God.

Jesus said to His disciples: *"...but you shall receive power when the Holy Spirit has come upon you; and you shall be My witnesses both in Jerusalem, and in all Judea and Samaria, and even to the remotest part of the earth." (Acts 1:8 NASB)*

My Blessing for You

May the Lord's Holy Spirit flow through you, filling every nook and cranny, meeting every need in your life.

May you know the height, breadth, width and depth of His love for you.

May you experience His tender mercies which are new every morning.

May His joy fill you and overflow through you onto others.

May others look at you and see His presence and glory.

May others hear the words of Christ as you speak blessings of encouragement and truth, words which are seasoned with grace.

May you look upon the hills of your city and notice that they are white and ripe for harvest.

May you not be ashamed of the gospel of Jesus Christ; ready, in season and out, to share the love of Christ with others.

In Jesus' Name, Amen.

Journal of My Journey with the Spoken Blessing

What will you do this week to serve as God's minister of reconciliation?

_____
_____
_____

Write a blessing that addresses a specific need in someone's life. Speak it.

_____
_____
_____

Identify needs within your church or body of believers of which you are a member. Write a blessing, then speak it over your fellow believers.

_____
_____
_____

Consider the city in which you live. Write, then speak that blessing over your city. Proclaim that blessing for 40 days.

_____
_____
_____

"The mouth of the righteous is a fountain of life....." (Proverbs 10:11 NASB)

Chapter Six
Assuming the Spiritual Posture to Bless

We assume our spiritual posture as we kneel at the feet of Jesus.

> *Come, let us worship and bow down; Let us kneel before the LORD our Maker.*
>
> *For He is our God, And we are the people of His pasture, and the sheep of His hand.*
>
> *Today, if you would hear His voice, Do not harden your hearts...*
> (Psalm 95:6-7 NASB)

In this passage, the Hebrew word used for *worship* is *shachah* which was not used in the general sense of worship, but specifically to *bow down*, to *prostrate oneself* as an act of respect before a superior being. This honor was not only to superiors, but also to equals, but especially in worshipping a deity. It *meant to honor God with prayers.* It was *a way of showing submission.*

The Hebrew word used for *bow down* is *kara*. It is defined: to *bend* (the knees), to *kneel down*, to *sink down*, to afflict, to grieve, to writhe in pain, to cower.

With an attitude of submission and honor and in a posture of humility, the worshipper would, also, *barak---kneel down, bless, praise, be blessed,*

The Spoken Blessing I: A Spiritual Posture

pray to, invoke, ask a blessing. Yes, when we are worshipping in the Lord's presence, we do praise and bless Him. (Strong's Concordance)

> *I will extol [rum] Thee, my God, O King; and I will bless [barak] Thy name [shem] forever and ever. Every day will I bless Thee, And I will praise Thy name forever and ever.*
>
> *One generation shall praise Thy works to another, and shall declare Thy mighty acts.* (Psalm 145:1-2,4 NASB)

With a posture of worship and honor we *extol* our God and King. We *raise Him above* everyone, every situation, every challenge in our lives. We *bless* and *praise* His honor, authority and character. Before the next generation, we explain His victory, power and strength. Parents, grandparents, uncles, aunts, teachers, pastors, all believers are called to honor our God and King before others.

When we are in His presence, we are blessed.

> "The LORD is good to all: And His mercies are over all His works." "Thou dost open Thy hand, And dost satisfy the desire of every living thing."
> (Psalm 145:9,16 NASB)

Speaking blessings over others can occur as a result of worshipping our Lord and King.

When we remain in His presence, we can invoke or put His name upon a situation or person, asking for and releasing a blessing. We bless others, in His Name. As we bless others, we celebrate and give glory to our God. Speaking blessings over others can occur as a result of *worshipping our LORD and King.*

> *The LORD is near to all who call upon Him, To all who call upon Him in truth. He will fulfill the desire of those who fear Him; He will also hear their cry, and will save them.*
>
> *My mouth will speak the praise [tehillah] of the LORD; And all flesh will bless His holy name forever and ever."*
> (Psalm 145:18,19,21 NASB)

Tehillah is the Hebrew word used in verse 21 which is translated as *praise*. The meaning of *Tehillah* is laudation, a *song of praise, glory*, praiseworthiness, *deeds which are worthy of praise*.

Tehillah is traceable to *halal* which means to *boast*, to *celebrate*, to *cause to shine*. The phrase *hallelujah* calls for *giving the glory to God*. As we bless others, we bring to light the faithfulness of God. We celebrate His goodness and boast in who He is. Our blessings affirm God's deeds which are worthy to be praised.

When our triune being: body, soul and spirit, worships the Lord, the fullness of His love and mercy fills us to overflowing. It is from this overflow that our hearts are stirred with compassion to encourage, support and bless others---as Jesus blesses us. When we bless others *for His sake* or *in His Name*, we identify and help them acknowledge that He is the only one worthy to be entrusted with our lives and our future.

"Do not trust in princes, in mortal man, in whom there is no salvation."

"How blessed is he whose help is the God of Jacob, whose hope is in the LORD his God;" (Psalm 146:3,5 NASB)

"Let them praise the name of the LORD, For His name alone is exalted; His glory is above earth and heaven." (Psalm 148:13 NASB)

Our lives must keep a posture of humility and an attitude of submission and honor before the One who blesses.

We must establish a deep-seated and settled trust in Him.

In Psalm 91, there is a beautiful relationship expressed between the worshipper and his LORD: *"He who dwells in the shelter of the Most High will abide in the shadow of the Almighty. I will say to the LORD, 'My refuge and my fortress, My God, in whom I trust!'"* (Psalm 91:1,2 NASB)

God responds to the worshipper:

> *Because he has loved [chashaq] Me, therefore I will deliver him; I will set him securely on high, because he has known My name. He will call upon Me, and I will answer him; I will be with him in trouble;*

The Spoken Blessing I: A Spiritual Posture

I will rescue him, and honor him. With a long life I will satisfy him, And let him behold My salvation. (Psalm 91:14-16 NASB)

In God's response, He reveals several cause and effect relationships:

Cause	Effect
1. *person sets his love on* God	1. God delivers him
2. person knows God's names (has personal experience with and knowledge of God)	2. God establishes him with authority
3. person calls upon God	3. God hears his plea and answers him
4. person is in trouble	4. God is with him, not leaving him
5. person needs help	5. God rescues him
6. person needs edifying	6. God honors him
7. person wants to live for God and wants His sovereignty in his life	7. God fulfills his desires
8. person wants to see His salvation	8. God shows him His help, deliverance, salvation, victory, welfare, prosperity

When a person *loves (chashaq)* God, he is attached to Him, he takes pleasure and delight in Him, he is joined together with Him, cleaving and adhering to Him. It is a love that will not let go. Thus, if this person is so close to God, he can't help but be delivered, rescued and extricated from a *hot spot*. Jesus escaped a crowd who wanted to kill Him, because His time to die had not yet come (John 8:59; 10:31,39). I do not disregard the martyrs (past, present and future) who gave (and will give) their earthly lives to serve our heavenly King. As Stephen was being stoned, he looked upward into the presence of His Lord. His Lord extricated or drew him out of that situation. Stephen's earthly body died, but his spirit soared into heaven (Acts 7:54-60). Even when we give our earthly lives for a heavenly purpose, it is not an indication that the enemy has won or that God has forsaken us. Just the contrary: the enemy lost us at the precise moment when we gave our lives to Christ.

> *The giving of our lives occurs before the time of our physical death.*

"Greater love has no one than this, that one lay down his life for his friends." (John 15:13; I John 3:16 NASB)

Our love for Jesus, causes us to adhere to Him and do what He did---sacrifice Himself. When believers reach this level of consecration and love, they will bless and curse not their neighbor, letting all blessings flow.

Join with me in a prayer of repentance for not loving Jesus to this degree:

> *Lord Jesus, please forgive me for not loving You in the depths of my being. Please forgive me for wanting all Your goodness, mercy and grace without the total sacrifice of my life. Forgive me for presuming upon Your grace. Please forgive me for not adhering to and immersing myself in Your presence. Forgive me for allowing other things to take precedence in my life. Lord, I want to establish You as my life, my source, my sustenance, the One in Whom I trust for everything. Jesus, I humble and submit myself, all of me, to You. In Your Name, I pray. Amen.*

Oh, Father, teach us now, I pray. Teach us the humility and submissiveness of Jesus. Forgive me, Father, of all haughtiness in my spirit. I crucify the attitude of pride. Oh, Lord, let us become the oil that flows out of our broken, alabaster box. The oil that costs us everything---our entire life's earnings, everything we have built our lives upon---we pour it at Your feet. Take it all, Lord, so we have nothing left of ourselves so You can fill us up with only You, Your nature and character. A broken and contrite heart, You will not despise.

Humility, submission and love for God provides knowledge of Him, experiencing the fullest dimensions of His name, His character.

Yada is to know. If we *know* the names of God, we have spent much time at His feet and in His presence. We have walked and talked with Him. We have watched His ways and observed His workings. We have experienced His different names and know that we can call upon those attributes when in need.

The Spoken Blessing I: A Spiritual Posture

Sit at the feet of Jesus in quiet repose, carefully weighing and considering His words of instruction and wisdom. Repose refers to resting from work, travel, exercise, etc. It means that you are depending upon or relying on someone or something beyond yourself. Your mind is at peace and free from the worries of the world.

As you discipline your mind to overcome the worries of the world, may Jesus reward you by sharing His intimacies with you.

"Every violent thug is despised by the Lord, but every tender lover finds friendship with God and will hear his intimate secrets." (Proverbs 3:32 TPT)

Allow His truth, His life-depositing words, to become the authority over your life, the rule of your conduct. Join the ranks of those biblical giants who have assumed a similar posture:

"Then David the king went in and sat before the LORD and said, 'Who am I, O LORD God, and what is my house that Thou hast brought me this far?'" (I Chronicles 17:16 NASB)

Speaking of his heritage and thorough training, Paul declared:

> *I am a Jew, born in Tarsus of Cilicia but reared in this city. At the feet of Gamaliel I was educated according to the strictest care in the Law of our fathers, being ardent [even a zealot] for God, as all of you are today.* (Acts 22:3 AMP)

Allow your heart to be stirred to embrace His joys, His sorrows, His goals, His Kingdom vision.

Seek the broader dimensions of the teachings and parables of Jesus. Read between the lines. Dig deeper for the treasures hidden beneath the surface. Ask Jesus to explain His teachings to you.

> *Jesus used many parables such as these as he taught the people, and they learned according to their ability to understand. He never spoke to them without using parables, but would wait until they were alone before he explained their meanings to his disciples.*
> (Mark 4:33,34 TPT)

Value His gemstones of truth, examining their multi-faceted surfaces. Look into the light of His glory as did the Emmaus Road disciples. As they intently listened to their dinner guest explain the Scriptures, their demeanor changed, and their perspective of Jesus turned 180°. Allow your heart to be stirred to embrace His joys, His sorrows, His goals, His Kingdom vision. Faith in Jesus' eternal purpose was birthed within their hearts that night. After listening and learning from Jesus, these disciples' vision changed from being *near-sighted* to *far-sighted;* for they could see far into the future of God's Kingdom. They were comforted and encouraged by this new perspective; not allowing the present circumstances to discourage or hinder them.

Upon listening to Jesus, the Emmaus Road disciples openly expressed their faith in Him. Such faith pleases God. Two other disciples had spent time at the feet of Jesus: Mary and Martha. Mary and Martha expressed faith and expectation in Jesus as they called for His help when their beloved brother, Lazarus, was seriously ill. After the death of her brother, Martha heard of Jesus' arrival at Bethany. Martha arose from her weeping to greet her Lord and to openly confess who He was for her and for the world.

> *I have believed [I do believe] that You are the Christ [the Messiah, the Anointed One], the Son of God, [even He] Who was to come into the world. [It is for Your coming that the world has waited.]*
> (John 11:27 AMP)

We must remain humble and submissive to Him, honoring His omniscience.

Martha may not have understood Jesus' delay in coming to their aid, but she was not deterred from greeting Him with warm hospitality and affirmation of her faith in Him. Martha teaches us something very important here: when we call upon the name of Jesus, expecting Him to respond in a certain way, and He doesn't, we should not assume that we are being denied an answer or that He isn't interested in our concern. Our faith in Him should not suffer, nor be shaken. We should continue to openly confess, as Martha did, who Jesus is for us and to the world. Our prayers and our blessings should remain focused on Him, His nature and His purpose. As in the death of Lazarus and in the delay of Jesus' arrival, we must remember that God's ways are higher than ours, His understanding more complete, His timing more perfect. We must remain humble and submissive to Him, honoring His omniscience.

While in our finite minds and limited understanding of His ways, we may not grasp the totality of the *task at hand*, we can be confident that eternal destinies are being developed, and the Lord's salvation is being accomplished. Our belief in Him and outward confession of our faith will open *doors of opportunity* for us to witness the glory of God and for others to enter His Salvation.

... if you believe, you will see the glory of God...

Jesus said to her {Martha}, 'Did I not say to you, if you believe, you will see the glory of God?' And so they removed the stone. And Jesus raised His eyes, and said, 'Father, I thank Thee that Thou heardest Me. And I knew that Thou hearest Me always; but because of the people standing around I said it, that they may believe that Thou didst send Me.' And when He had said these things, He cried out with a loud voice, 'Lazarus, come forth.' He who had died came forth, bound hand and foot with wrappings, and his face was wrapped around with a cloth. Jesus said to them, 'Unbind him, and let him go.' Many therefore of the Jews, who had come to Mary and beheld what He had done, believed in Him. (John 11:40-45 NASB)

Trust God to operate within the fullest dimension of eternity.

To reveal the glory of God and for the work of salvation, Jesus delayed His response to His friends' call for help. Delay does not equate to denial. Take note that many Jews had come to comfort and mourn with Mary and Martha. These friends would have had no reason to be with Lazarus' sisters if Jesus had healed and rescued Lazarus from death. By delaying His arrival, *Jesus performed a resurrection miracle* before the eyes and hearts of these *Jewish friends which led to their belief in Him*. Trust God to operate within the fullest dimension of eternity. Our faith must not be shaken, but confident in God's perfect plan of action within our world. Faith exercised and expressed can result in the resurrection of *dead* areas within lives as we release blessings of truth and life over people. We can *unbind them* and *free them* from the grave cloths of defeat and discouragement. *New life*, new hope, new optimism will *replace* death and *decay*. Their attitudes and outlook will no longer *stink*, but will emit the sweet fragrance of the presence of the Lord ruling and reigning in their lives.

Recall with me the story in Mark 11 that describes Jesus cursing the fig tree and His disciples marveling that His words carried such power. He began a valuable lesson which can assist us in assuming the spiritual posture for speaking blessings.

"And Jesus answered saying to them, 'Have faith in God.'"
(Mark 11:22 NASB)

Faith is the English translation of the Greek word, *pistis,* which means *being persuaded; faith; believe.* In general, it implies such a *knowledge of,* assent to, and *confidence in* certain *divine truths,* especially those of the Gospel, *as produces good works.*

That definition tells me that our faith in God should result in doing good. Consider the following scriptures which remind us of the importance of our lively, active faith in Christ:

"Do not withhold good from those to whom it is due, when it is in your power to do it." (Proverbs 3:27 NASB)

"... I will show you my faith by my works." (James 2:18 NASB)

Pistis relates to miraculous faith or that faith in Christ to which, when the Gospel was first spread, the gift of miracles was added. The working of miracles became an additional consequence of an active, power-filled faith.

Paul prayed that such a faith would be *developed* within the Colossian believers:

> *We have not ceased to pray for you and to ask that you may be filled with the knowledge of His will in all spiritual wisdom and understanding, so that you may walk in a manner worthy of the Lord,*

to please Him in all respects, bearing fruit in every good work and increasing in the knowledge of God; strengthened with all power, according to His glorious might, for the attaining of all steadfastness and patience; joyously giving thanks to the Father, who has qualified us to share in the inheritance of the saints in light.

(Colossians 1:9-12 NASB)

To assume the posture to use *the Spoken Blessing* effectively, we need to:

1. *"be filled with the knowledge of His will in all spiritual wisdom and understanding"* Just as Jacob spoke appropriate blessings over his sons, we are to seek and listen for wisdom from God's Spirit as we bless others.

2. *"walk in a manner worthy of the Lord"* Bring God honor by redirecting someone's focus and attention back to Him.

3. *"please Him in all respects"* Be obedient to God's word as He instructs us to bless and not curse people. Share the cup of forgiveness. And do not neglect doing good and sharing, for with such sacrifices God is pleased (Hebrews 13:16 NASB).

4. *"bear fruit in every good work"* The fruit of the righteous is a tree of life, and he who is wise wins souls (Proverbs 11:30 NASB).

5. *"increase in the knowledge of God"* As we study and seek to understand the nature of God, we will know how He desires to bless others. Study Jesus. Carefully examine His interactions with people and consider the outcome. Ask Him to relate each situation to your life.

6. *"be strengthened with all power, according to His glorious might"* As God did special miracles through the hands of Paul (Acts 19:11), He will enable us to release and build up greater measures of faith and works within others.

7. *"attain all steadfastness and patience"* We must press on toward the goal for the prize of the upward call of God in Christ Jesus (Philippians 3:14). Our blessings should encourage others to do the same. We are to become secure and established in our faith, patient in our daily walk.

8. *"joyously give thanks to the Father"* Our blessings should remind fellow believers to bless, praise and thank our heavenly Father (Psalm 145).

Take note of the last phrase of Colossians 1:12 (NASB): *"who has qualified us to share in the inheritance of the saints in light."* The act of confessing with our mouths that Jesus is our Lord allows us to step into an eternal inheritance. We must express our faith in Him.

> *That if you confess with your mouth Jesus as Lord, and believe in your heart that God raised Him from the dead, you shall be saved; for with the heart man believes, resulting in righteousness, and with the mouth he confesses, resulting in salvation.* (Romans 10:9-10 NASB)

I am continually reminded of how our choice to believe in Christ and our willingness to confess that faith affects, not only ourselves, but others. On many occasions, I have felt prompted by God's Spirit to speak a blessing over someone in our store. Most often, I witness a visible change in their countenance. Many times, they will say: "Thank you, I needed that." Their responses are not casual or superficial, but filled with gratitude. I can see it in their eyes as they look at me with a different intensity. By God's Spirit, I minister to their spirit. Our spirits are eternal: they existed before we were given an earthly body and will exist after this earthly body dies. This underscores the importance of calling *deep unto deep*, spirit summoning spirit. Our eternity, their eternity lies ahead.

Recall the consequence of blessing others as identified in I Peter 3:9 (NASB), *"for you were called for the very purpose that you might inherit a blessing."* Repeatedly God's word reiterates the correlation between our actions and our eventual inheritance.

> *"Whatever you do, do your work heartily, as for the Lord rather than for men; knowing that from the Lord you will receive the reward of the inheritance. It is the Lord Christ whom you serve."* (Colossians 3:23-24 NASB)

As we grow in our understanding of God's message regarding *the Spoken Blessing*, we must translate it into faith-filled action. Such action is identified in Mark 11:23 (NASB):

"Truly I say to you, whoever says [G2036] to this mountain, 'Be taken up and cast into the sea...'"

Epo is the Hebrew word for *says*. Strong's Concordance provides this definition: *"to speak or say (by word or writting): - answer, bid, bring word, call, command, grant, say (on), speak, tell."* A person must speak blessings with authority. We must be confident in God's power who works within us, namely, His Holy Spirit. We must recognize the significance and importance of our work here on earth, in this lifetime, as it relates to the future: individually and corporately. We must embrace a larger picture that incorporates eternity. Please read Dr. Bruce Wilkinson's *A Life God Rewards---Why Everything You Do Today Matters Forever* and gain a new perspective on eternity.

We cannot be spineless men and women of the faith. In fact, those are opposing ideas. If we are committed believers and confess faith in the Lord, we will walk uprightly, holding our heads up high, shoulders firmly set, backbones straight and strong. As we gain the revelation of God's Kingdom living within us and the Kingdom in which we shall live, we will rule and reign with Jesus; confident and assertive.

Each of us needs the other in our service to the Lord.

Why is grabbing hold of this *larger picture* so vital to our *pressing on toward the goal for the prize?* Life has its *pressing* moments or seasons. Olives produce oil and grapes produce juice when they are pressed and crushed. *Crushing circumstances* are not comfortable. But, as we are *pressed,* we must *press* on towards a deeper, more intimate relationship with our Lord. As God gives us an understanding of what is happening and why, we must respond with submission and obedience. In honor and reverence to Jesus, we can take our *pressed oil* or *extracted juice* and pour it on His feet. There are Christians who become angry at God for different reasons. These people refuse to be *crushed* for the sake of spiritual growth and a deeper walk. Their hearts are hardened to His Spirit and their necks are stiffened to His correction. They become *bitter* instead of *better.* They choose to focus on their present, instead of their future. Cal and I have walked through *crushing* times. On our knees and before the Lord, we have *panned* for the golden nuggets of truth, allowing the water of His word to wash away the dirt and debris of disappointments. Our faith in God's BIGGER picture was at the forefront of our minds and hearts. Yes, we had to repent and allow Holy Spirit to accomplish His sanctifying work.

We had friends who prayed for us, blessed and exhorted us in our faith. No man is an island. When asked for instruction in prayer, Jesus stressed to His disciples the idea of the community of believers: *"Our Father who art in heaven... give us this day... forgive us... as we also have... do not lead us... deliver us..."* (Matthew 6:9-13 NASB). Each of us needs the other in our service to the Lord.

We are the Body of Christ. Our physical bodies must remain aligned to function properly. Many health problems develop when we get out of alignment. There are highly trained, medical professionals who help us realign our skeletal structures for optimal health. We can assist one another, within the Body of Christ, to become spiritually realigned and to maintain this proper posture.

We need this spiritual posture to enable us to rule and reign with Jesus.

Jesus equipped His disciples for His kingdom work:

> *And He called the twelve together, and gave them power and authority over all the demons and to heal diseases. And He sent them out to proclaim the kingdom of God, and to perform healing.*
> (Luke 9:1-2 NASB)

There was an impartation of power and authority from Jesus to His disciples. Jesus challenged them to think and see beyond what they had witnessed while serving Him:

> *Truly, truly I say to you, he who believes in Me, the works that I do shall he do also; and greater works than these shall he do; because I go to the Father: And whatever you ask in My name, that will I do, that the Father may be glorified in the Son. If you ask Me anything in My name, I will do it.* (John 14:12-14 NASB)

We are to *have faith* in the majesty of God and *the magnitude* of His Kingdom work. Jesus' disciples had witnessed healing, deliverance, resurrection, blessing, re-creation, compassion, mercy, forgiveness, etc. Jesus expected and called His disciples to exponentially multiply His work. We are called to do no less.

The Spoken Blessing I: A Spiritual Posture

A side note of interest: Jesus explained to His disciples: *"Whatsoever you ask in my name that will I do"* (John 14:13). He expressed the importance of their prayers being conformable to His nature and character; to the actions His disciples observed Him doing while on earth. Our blessings should follow suit. As we speak blessings based upon God's word, He will respond to those blessings. He desires to execute His power-packed word within the lives of people.

Let's continue with our original passage found in Mark 11:22-23 (NASB):

"Have faith in God. Truly I say to you, whoever says to this mountain, 'Be taken up and cast into the sea,' and does not doubt in his heart,"

Doubt means: to be distinguished or divided in one's mind.

Doubting or not doubting is related to our confidence in God and in His ultimate will for our lives and those of others. *"Therefore, do not throw away your confidence, which has a great reward."* (Hebrews 10:35 NASB). Jesus addressed the doubt and faithlessness in His disciple, Thomas, who would not believe in His resurrection until he could see and touch Jesus in person. *"Because you have seen Me, have you believed? Blessed are they who did not see, and yet believed"* (John 20:29 NASB). God truly desires and is eager to encourage His divine nature and image to be multiplied across the world. Doubt can have no place in us. It cannot hold any power over our faith.

Continuing with Mark 11:23 (NASB): *"and does not doubt in his heart, but believes that what he says is going to happen."*

Pisteuo is the Greek word which is translated as *believes*. *Pisteuo* means "to have faith (in, upon, or with respect to, a person or thing), that is, credit; by implication to entrust (especially one's spiritual well being to Christ): believe (-r), commit (to trust), put in trust with."[6]

Once again, *faith is the focal point*. Being confident in what we believe is essential. Confidence has its reward. Jesus questioned His disciples about the basis of their faith in Him:

> *He said to them, 'But who do you say that I am?' And Simon Peter answered and said, "Thou art the Christ, the Son of the living God."*

> *And Jesus answered and said to him, "Blessed are you, Simon Barjona, because flesh and blood did not reveal this to you, but My Father who is in heaven. And I also say to you that you are Peter and upon this rock I will build My church; and the gates of Hades shall not overpower it."* (Matthew 16:15-18 NASB)

Simon Peter was *blessed, makarios, filled up, fully satisfied* by the spiritual insight deposited into his understanding. The Father saw a receptive heart into which He could share His intimate mysteries. This gift of understanding of the identity of God's Son was the cornerstone upon which Jesus Christ would build His Church---His Ekklesia. As Jesus recognized the spiritual insight given to Peter, He knew that there was no doubt within Peter's heart or mind. Peter was able to state, with confidence, his belief that Jesus was The Anointed One, the Christ. Jesus knew He could accomplish His kingdom work within a life so totally convinced of this fact. With this confidence, we are to speak blessings based upon the words of Christ. Every believer has an anointing given by the presence of the Spirit of Christ.

> *"But you have been anointed by [you hold a sacred appointment from, you have been given an unction from] the Holy One, and you all know [the Truth] or you know all things."* (I John 2:20 AMP)

Webster's Dictionary explains the word *unction*: *"a quality or manner of utterance, especially in dealing with religious themes, that is fervent and earnest, or meant to express or arouse deep spiritual feeling."* As the Spirit of the Lord stirs within us, teaching, directing and moving us in His truth and compassion, we will not be able to keep our mouths from declaring His blessings upon people. As we are trained by His Spirit, fervent words of encouragement will be spoken with faith that it will happen. Our words of faith spoken over someone else will serve to encourage us.

> *"So faith comes from hearing, and hearing by the word of Christ."*
> (Romans 10:17 NASB)

Life Application:

There are times when a child is struggling with an issue and the parents feel his pain. When the parents speak blessings over the child, parents and child are strengthened because they are reminded of God's presence and interest. All are reassured that it is God's loving-kindness and faithfulness that will provide victory over the challenge.

> *May you watch as God does exceedingly abundantly beyond all that you ask or think, according to the power of His Spirit who works within you.*
>
> *May God's favor surround you like a shield.*
>
> *May the Lord be your Good Shepherd, caring and providing for your every need.*
>
> *May you call upon the name of Jesus when you need help.*
>
> *In Jesus' Name, Amen.*

If a spouse, friend or co-worker has been harassed by demeaning words spoken by others, it is vital to their victory for you to continually speak blessings of affirmation and encouragement. Old thoughts and perspectives must be washed away, and new outlooks must be imparted. Unfortunately, there are times when family members, friends and work associates berate our loved ones. Those repetitive harsh judgments often create a defeated and inferior mentality within our spouse or friend. Those condemning words must be confronted with God's truth. By the authority and command of Christ, we are to love others. On the home front, husbands are to *agapao* their wives. They are to *love* their wives, *indicating a direction of the husband's will.* Remember the words of Paul found in Ephesians 5:25-30 (NASB):

> *Husbands, love your wives, just as Christ also loved the church and gave Himself up for her; that He might sanctify her, having cleansed her by the washing of water with the word, that He might present to Himself the church in all her glory, having no spot or wrinkle or any such thing; but that she should be holy and blameless. So husbands ought also to love their own wives as their own bodies. He who loves*

his own wife loves himself; for no one ever hated his own flesh, but nourishes and cherishes it, just as Christ also does the church, because we are members of His body.

Husbands are to extend great compassion to their wives, discovering how to lovingly encourage them in all the seasons of life through which they walk. Husbands and wives must be careful not to destroy each other with name-calling and destructive words. Husbands and wives are to place great value on each other recognizing that both are important to the Ekklesia---Christ's Church.

Wives, we must learn how to forgive the offenses that come from our husbands. Now, be honest. Offenses from our husbands are, often, some of the hardest ones to *get over*. A key element to our emotional, physical, and spiritual health is directly connected to our *forgiveness*. Our *forgiveness* is directly related to our being able to bless and not curse our husbands. Our blessing them affects our inheritance in eternity.

Fellow wives and fellow mothers, we have a great responsibility to the building up of our homes: *"The wise woman builds her house, But the foolish tears it down with her own hands."* (Proverbs 14:1 NASB)

The *building up* or the *tearing down* is in the *power of our hands and our mouths*. Our husbands need affirmation. They need our admiration according to Dr. Willard F. Harley, Jr., author of *His Needs, Her Needs*. Dr. Harley suggests that "when a woman tells a man she thinks he's wonderful, that inspires him to achieve more. He sees himself as capable of handling new responsibilities and perfecting skills far above those of his present level. That inspiration helps him prepare for the responsibilities of life. Admiration not only motivates, it also rewards the husband's existing achievements. For some men---those with fragile self-images---admiration also helps them believe in themselves. While criticism causes men to become defensive, admiration energizes and motivates them. A man expects---and needs his wife to be his most enthusiastic fan. He draws confidence from her support and can usually achieve far more with her encouragement."

Wives, our husbands need our blessings, our faith-filled words of God's truth spoken over, around, before and behind them. Even when we speak about them to others, our words must always honor and esteem them.

Our husbands should be able to safely trust us with their honor and their every need as is described in Proverbs 31:11-12 (AMP):

> *The heart of her husband trusts in her confidently and relies on and believes in her securely, so that he has no lack of [honest] gain or need of [dishonest] spoil. She comforts, encourages, and does him only good as long as there is life within her.*

May I share with you the commentary on Proverbs 31:10-31 provided by e-Sword X, a Bible study application that I recommend:

> *It is in the home-place that the man's strength is gathered for public life. The woman in the home communicates the inspiration and strength which make him "known in the gates." Her secret, unobtrusive loyalty, counsel, and thrift inspire a growing depth of appreciation; so that the man who chose her in the spring will say of her amid the snows of age, "Other women may be good and true, but 'thou excellest them all.'"*

Wives, our words can affect who our husbands are and who they shall become. Let us carefully consider God's perspective concerning our husbands. Do not condone or agree with attitudes which condemn or demean *husbands* or *men*. We must not remain silent when other females criticize the male gender. They are attacking the image of God.

We are to honor the image of Christ that dwells within our husbands and our children.

Speaking blessings over our husbands honors them as the co-laborers in Christ that they are. We are to honor the image of Christ that dwells within our husbands *and* our children. As wives and mothers, we are to *build up our homes*. Dr. Harley identified that low self-esteem has been one of the most common problems his clients have had to overcome. He explained that this low self-esteem begins very early, in the home during childhood. This fact underlines the necessity of our watching our words, holding our tongues, even, biting them if necessary. Words can be so hurtful, but so comforting and motivating, when they are *seasoned with salt* (Colossians 4:6). Remember, salt is a *preservative*. We are to *preserve* our family's honor and image.

Likewise, we can (it is a choice we make) play an important role in the setting apart of fellow believers for the work of God's kingdom. We can remind them of the authority that God has over their lives and over His world. We can challenge others to reach higher; to dig deeper, discovering the richer elements of life. We can extend compassion for their failures, while exhorting them to a purer walk of holiness. Cleansing one's mind and sanctifying one's thoughts can take time and may require repetition. There is a joy and a reward for serving others.

Jesus said, *"For whoever gives you a cup of water to drink because of your name as followers of Christ, truly I say to you, he shall not lose his reward."* (Mark 9:41 NASB)

The principle of the cleansing and restorative power of God's word is evident and profound. People need to hear who they are in Christ. We have the ability and the anointing to build up and establish a firm foundation of faith, hope and love within others as we speak blessings over them.

God has placed a seed of greatness within every person. We can help it grow and develop into a tree of righteousness that bears good fruit. Jesus explained that when we pray, in a posture of worship, we must believe that we will receive our requests.

> *And Jesus answered them, "Have faith in God. Truly, I say to you, whoever says to this mountain, 'Be taken up and thrown into the sea,' and does not doubt in his heart, but believes that what he says will come to pass, it will be done for him."* (Mark 11:22,23 ESV)

It is imperative that we trust God to act on the behalf of others and ourselves. Trust God's word when it declares:

> *But just as it is written, 'things which eye has not seen and ear has not heard, and which have not entered the heart of man, all that God has prepared for those who love Him.' For to us God revealed them through the Spirit; for the Spirit searches all things, even the depths of God.* (I Corinthians 2:9-10 NASB)

Assuming the spiritual posture to bless others requires a humble and contrite heart, a heart filled with worship, a life totally submitted to Jesus' Lordship, faith in who He is, and confidence in the authority and power He has given you.

My Blessing for You

May you kneel at the feet of Jesus.

May you allow Him to take you by the hand, His omnipotent hand, and set your feet on the solid foundation of faith in Him. As He causes your faith to flourish, may you take steps to accomplish His mighty work for the furtherance of His Kingdom.

May you walk with a heart of submission, operating with an understanding of your authority and command to bless.

May you continually bless the God of your salvation, encouraging others to do the same.

In Jesus' Name, Amen.

Journal of My Journey with the Spoken Blessing

What do you need to learn at the feet of Jesus?

What area in your life has yet to be totally submitted to His authority?

Identify the level of trust in God that you desire to assume. What must you do to get there?

Describe the effect God has recently had on your life. Explain the situation and His response.

The Spoken Blessing I: A Spiritual Posture

Recount a situation in which God's response to you appeared to be delayed. When and how did He answer?

_____
_____
_____

This week, how will you show others your faith by your works?

_____
_____
_____
_____

"And my God shall supply all your needs according to His riches in glory in Christ Jesus." (Philippians 4:19 NASB)

Chapter Seven
Interning with the Spoken Blessing

Are you ready to begin using *the Spoken Blessing*? Are you willing to put your approach to life to the test? Carefully consider the following story from Luke 7:

> *And it came about soon afterwards, that He went to a city called Nain; and His disciples were going along with Him, accompanied by a large multitude. Now as He approached the gate of the city, behold, a dead man was being carried out, the only son of his mother, and she was a widow; and a sizeable crowd from the city was with her. And when the Lord saw her, He felt compassion for her; and said to her, "Do not weep." And He came up and touched the coffin; and the bearers came to a halt. And He said, "Young man, I say to you, arise!" And the dead man sat up, and began to speak. And Jesus gave him back to his mother. And fear gripped them all, and they began glorifying God, saying, "A great prophet has arisen among us!" and "God has visited His people!"* (Luke 7:11-16 NASB)

He did not want to fix a problem.

There were two crowds that day. The atmosphere around each was distinctively different. There was an air of excitement and anticipation surrounding Jesus and His disciples. A cloud of doom and gloom hovered over the mourners. If we had been there, of which crowd would we have been a part? Which outlook on life do we embrace? Are we an excited, expectant, faith-filled follower of the Lord? Or are we forlorn, hopeless, and dejected? Are we in a *survival mode*? Does our future appear as bleak as this widow's? This woman was not only a widow, but her last means of provision had just died. Her future did not appear promising. We could imagine that the winds of despair were blinding her from seeing her future in a positive way. Her visual impairment was caused by a *blurred* and *downcast* view of life. But then, God appeared on the scene. God in the flesh, our Lord Jesus, was moved with compassion. The word, *compassion*, indicates that the *total person* feels deep pity. Jesus' entire nature responded to this widow. He did not want to fix a problem. He wanted to show how much the Father loves and cares for widows. Restoration was needed. Jesus did more than restore life and provision in the natural sense. Awe and reverence for His Heavenly Father gripped this crowd, not just the widow. Their spiritual focus was changed. Their awareness of God's working among them was heightened. Hope was restored; hope was multiplied.

Will Jesus find it necessary to say to us:

> *Stop wailing over the disappointments and hardships in your life. Look to your heavenly Father who loves you and extends His lovingkindness to you. He will supply your daily bread. Great is His faithfulness.*

When we view life through the eyes of Jesus, we can see His light of truth flooding our future. The hearts that have been darkened by doubt and despair can choose to allow His fountain of life to flood through them, washing away the death and decay of sadness. As we speak blessings with great compassion, we can touch the dead areas and disheartened emotions within someone with God's word of life. We can assist them in viewing their life through the eyes of Jesus.

When we view life through the eyes of Jesus...

Jesus said: *"I came that they may have and enjoy life, and have it in abundance (to the full, till it overflows)."* (John 10:10 AMP)

Do you want this 'abundant life?' The coming Messiah declared through the voice of the prophet: *"For the Lord GOD helps Me, Therefore I am not disgraced; Therefore, I have set My face like flint, And I know that I shall not be ashamed."* (Isaiah 50:7 NASB)

We walk in the direction of our focus.

To *set*, suwm, means to *establish*, to *erect*, to *plant*, to *put*, to *appoint*; to *set aside for a special purpose*. If our *face is set*, it is *firmly focused*---focused on our God in whom we trust. We walk in the direction of our focus. We will not be *ashamed*, buwsh, *disappointed*, *deceived* or *confused*. We will not suffer the shame of utter defeat. God is our very present help in times of trouble. The fiery trials of life must not distract us or force us into a lowly *survival mode* of thinking and speaking. We must not allow those trials to interfere with God's purpose for our lives and His plans for others. Psalm 23:1 declares that the LORD is our Shepherd, we shall not want. That important principle is the launching pad for our faith. He shall accomplish exceedingly abundantly more than we could ever ask or think (Ephesians 3:20). That's the baseline of our lives. Our authority, dominion and power in His Name, supersedes the basics of life. We *are* overcomers by the Blood of the Lamb! Our life has a purpose and it's *not just to survive.*

Even when Job lost his sons and daughters, servants, livestock, and even his health, he "did not sin with his lips" (Job 2:10). He did not blame God, instead, Job worshipped God and blessed His name (Job 1:20-22).

As we set our face, focused on the Lord, we direct our mouth to speak blessings, not curses. We will become like David who explained his inward resolve: *"I have purposed that my mouth will not transgress."*
(Psalm 17:3 NASB)

David carefully considered and planned that his character and disposition would not violate God's law, nor go beyond it. When I say something that causes pain to others, I am indeed regretful. My remorse causes me to meditate on why I said what I did, trying to understand myself and my attitude, so I can make changes. I attempt to find the root of the problem. Remove the root, the bad fruit dries up. I must be very honest

The Spoken Blessing I: A Spiritual Posture

with myself; emotionally separated and analytical. When I have offended someone, I apologize and ask for their forgiveness. I truly desire the song of David to be in my heart and on my lips:

"Let the words of my mouth and the meditation of my heart Be acceptable in Thy sight, O LORD, my rock and my Redeemer." (Psalm 19:14 NASB)

How can we keep our way pure and acceptable in God's sight?

> *By keeping it according to Thy word. With all my heart I have sought Thee,*
> *Do not let me wander from Thy commandments. Thy word I have treasured in my heart,*
> *That I may not sin against Thee.* (Psalm 119:9-11 NASB)

Read the same passage in the Amplified Bible:

> *By taking heed and keeping watch [on himself] according to Your word [conforming his life to it]. With my whole heart have I sought You, inquiring for and of You and yearning for You; O let me not wander or step aside [either in ignorance or willfully] from Your commandments. Your word have I laid up in my heart, that I might not sin against You.*

To *wander*, shagah, is to *waver*, to *go astray*, to *err*, to *transgress*, to *cause to wander*, to *sin through ignorance*.[7]

One thing that causes us to stray away from God's commands is the inability to *fend off* evil talk.

To *fend off* is to *ward off, turn aside,* or *repel.* Recall that *evil talk* is full of *fear, doubt* and *unbelief.*

This is an area of sin into which many people *wander*. We listen to and agree with many attitudes and words of people who spew out negative, woe-filled expectations. Consider these examples: "Well, if it's not one thing, it's another." This is often spoken after several *bad* things have happened. "Everything happens to me in threes. I wonder what else is going to happen!" "I can't seem to do anything right." "He's never there when you need him." "Yeah, I always come up with the short end of the stick."

---

[7] *Lexicon to the Old and New Testaments,* edited by Spiros Zodhiates, Th.D., p. 1646, H7686

When we hear those words, we have a decision to make: do we chime in and add our own complaints about *life* or do we *repel* those words and attitudes? We must not accept them into our heart or embrace them as a way of life. We don't have to be rude with our response. Nobody likes a *holier than thou* approach. Remember, *"For all have sinned and fall short of the glory of God."* (Romans 3:23 NASB)

Even if our response includes a form of correction, it can be spoken with love. Offer them compassion for their pain or difficulty, then, offer hope in God's faithfulness to work things out. Many times, words of correction and encouragement are accepted, yet there are people who are *dead set* in their pessimistic attitudes. We must not become weary in our well doing. We must continue to sow seeds of righteousness and truth. We must also be teachable and correctable. There are times when we suffer *battle fatigue* and allow our emotions to control our attitudes and speech.

"Listen to counsel and accept discipline, That you may be wise the rest of your days." (Proverbs 19:20 NASB)

Be humble and teachable:

> *Come, you children, listen to me; I will teach you the fear of the LORD. Who is the man who desires life, And loves length of days that he may see good? Keep your tongue from evil, And your lips from speaking deceit. Depart from evil, and do good; Seek peace and pursue it.* (Psalm 34:11-14 NASB)

Most human beings would choose life over death and would add, not subtract, days to their life. They would prefer good things happening in their life, not bad. So, learning the "fear of the LORD" just might be a prudent thing to do!

First consider the meaning of the phrase: "the fear of the LORD." If one truly recognizes God as all-powerful, this will be reflected in his attitude and daily life in the form of reverence. The LORD is recognized as the sole Exerciser of power over the unwise and all mankind, as the Creator of the world and Disposer of life and death. If we walk 'in the fear of the LORD,' we will maintain a pious posture in which we perform practical functions in life. Have you ever met someone that is so *spiritual* with their *heads in the clouds* that they are of no *earthly good*? We must not be so. We must maintain our (vertical) relationship with the LORD, while we perform practical functions (horizontally) during our life on earth. That's what Jesus did.

As our spiritual posture conforms to the "fear of the LORD," we watch and protect our tongues from releasing hurtful words. Why, "protect?" Our witness for the Lord must be protected. Our injurious words can mar our testimony for God.

Our injurious words can mar our testimony for God.

We guard our hearts from harboring a negative attitude towards God. Our speech can promote honesty and integrity or deceitfulness and falsehood. What we choose will direct the course of our life, the length of our days and the good we will experience. When we refuse to accept inferior standards and choose to assume an upright posture, we will "do good."

Daily, we will anticipate, even ask God for, opportunities to speak the peace of Jesus over someone's life. We will be zealous in our speaking blessings for the benefit of others. We will hear from the throne room of God how to declare His will and way for others.

Declare this aloud:

> *I will set my face like flint upon the Lord. I will focus my eyes upon the Author and Finisher of my faith. I will declare God's life-depositing word over myself and others. I choose, this day, to serve the Lord with gladness, with a renewed and right spirit within me. In Jesus' Name, Amen.*

With great confidence in who God is and what He has equipped and called us to do, we are prepared to speak and declare blessings over others. We must ask God's Spirit to help us recognize opportunities to bless. Once we encounter the need, then we ask Him for the appropriate words of Christ. He will not disappoint us. He will be there to answer us because it is His desire to bless as He operates through us.

Raising children provides many opportunities for blessing them. When our youngest son, David, was five, he was overpowered by a fear of death and destruction. This occurred as he heard Cal and me discussing a natural gas leak at my parents' home. We carefully explained, trying not to instill fear, but fear grabbed hold of David's mind and spirit. For nights, I prayed and blessed him with confidence in the Lord's protection.

David, may the Lord protect you from all evil.

May He protect your soul: your mind, will and emotions.

May the Lord guard your going out and your coming in from this time forth and forever more.

In Jesus' Name, Amen.

I affirmed God's protection over him. This allowed David to witness my confidence in God. Remember the importance of protecting the witness of our mouths. Our children *need* to observe our confidence in the Lord, in day-to-day situations.

As I mentioned in an earlier chapter, there are times at church when someone asks me to pray with them. I do pray with them, *and* I bless them. I differentiate between the two as I assume different postures for them. I compare these spiritual postures with physical ones. To accomplish different tasks, such as bending to weed a garden, stooping to retrieve a dropped object, standing to help someone, we adjust our physical posture and position. We adjust to accomplish something. Likewise, in the spiritual realm, we assume various postures to execute different spiritual tasks, i.e.: expressing reverence to God, exercising faith, extending compassion, offering petitions to God, taking authority over the enemy, delivering God's timely message, teaching and preaching the gospel of Jesus Christ. The shift occurs as God's Spirit directs. He directs according to the task at hand. God's plans will be accomplished, here in earth, as they are in heaven.

We assume various postures to execute different spiritual tasks...

Consider this example: you converse with your child or an employee. Later, you assume an authoritative position and instruct them to do something. You are communicating, yet, with a different posture or relational position. Your spiritual posture with speaking blessings is one of authority, dominion and power; that which is given to you by the Lord to speak forth His word, trusting Him to perform it (Jeremiah 1:12 NASB).

Speaking blessings over others requires an unwavering confidence in God. With God, all things are possible (Matthew 19:26). Is there anything too hard for the Lord (Genesis 18:14)? There is no limit to His goodness, mercy and grace. When we confess Jesus' victory over troubling situations and believe in our hearts that life and a future reign over death and destruction, then we will be delivered out of those oppressive challenges. We will witness God's majesty prevailing. We will convey our faith to others as we assume a posture of faith.

Read Romans 10:8-10 (ESV):

> *But what does it say? "The word is near you, in your mouth and in your heart" (that is, the word of faith that we proclaim); because, if you confess with your mouth that Jesus is Lord and believe in your heart that God raised him from the dead, you will be saved. For with the heart one believes and is justified, and with the mouth one confesses and is saved.*

Every day we experience the benefits His Salvation. We proclaim the word of faith that originate in our hearts and is expressed through our mouths.

Read Romans 10:11 in The Passion Translation: *"For the Scriptures encourage us with these words: 'Everyone who believes in him will never be disappointed.'"*

Jesus does not disappoint. He can be trusted. We must convey our trust to others. We must help others call upon and apply Jesus' name over their lives and their circumstances.

Read Romans 10:13-15 in The Passion Translation:

> *And it's true: "Everyone who calls on the name of the Lord Yahweh will be rescued and experience new life."*
>
> *How then will they call on him in whom they have not believed? And how are they to believe in him of whom they have never heard? And how are they to hear without someone preaching? And how can the message be proclaimed if messengers have yet to be sent? That's why*

the Scriptures say: "How welcome is the arrival of those proclaiming the joyful news of peace and of good things to come!"

We are to be a bearer of good tidings of great joy which shall be for all the people (Luke 2:10). We are to serve God as messengers just as the angels delivered His message to the lowliest shepherds. There are many people around us who are functioning in a *lowly* state of faith. They need our message of hope, faith and love.

Clearly, speaking blessings over others requires an unwavering confidence in God.

So, let all blessings flow. These ideas may help your creativity. Holy Spirit will direct the rest.

1. The next time a telemarketer calls your house, listen to their promotional speech, then ask them if you can ask a question. Inquire if they are a believer in the Lord Jesus, if He is their Savior. Then, follow Holy Spirit's leading. If they are a believer, ask if you could bless their day, or work, or family. I have done this on the phone! One day, I was explaining my frustration with a company's lack of response, when the salesperson began listing all the difficulties that her company had suffered. Following the Spirit's leading, I asked if I could bless her. She said, "Hold on a minute." When the sales lady returned to the phone, she explained that she had turned on the speaker so her entire sales force could listen to my blessing! Now that is God's kind of multiplication: not just one person, but many were blessed! The eyes of many were refocused on God.

If the telemarketer is not a believer, express God's love for them and the eternal life He offers them. A possible blessing would be:

"May the Lord bless you with His presence, allowing you to see Him in all His glory.

May His truth touch your heart and comfort your soul.

In Jesus' Name, Amen."

The Spoken Blessing I: A Spiritual Posture

2. Bless your children in their *going out* and their *coming in*. Before your children leave for school, speak a blessing over them. When they are doing their homework, or studying for a test, release a blessing over their efforts.

May the Lord cause you to prosper and excel in all that you do.

May His favor surround you as a shield.

May you take joy in what you are asked to do.

May what you do bring honor to the Lord.

In Jesus' Name, Amen.

May God's Spirit instruct and direct your studying.

May He give you 'Holy Spirit highlights,' showing you what to study.

May your memory be blessed and increased.

May you make quick application of the information you study to the questions on your test.

May the peace of our Lord Jesus guard your heart and your mind.

In Jesus' Name, Amen.

3. When you leave a phone message, bless the listener. Picture this: you return home, after a hard day at work, turn on the voice mail and hear someone speaking a blessing over you. It's like a cup of cool, refreshing water to a dry, parched throat. The refreshment of God's word brings life and restoration, encouragement and love.

Hello, my friend. I won't be able to attend your party, but I would like to speak a blessing over your efforts.

May the Lord reward your work and your wages be full from the Lord, the God of Israel, under whose wings you have sought refuge.

May God give you wisdom and understanding in the administration of your work.

May He cause your hands to prosper.

May you never cease to bless and praise the Lord!

In Jesus' Name, Amen.

4. You may have family members or friends who don't live near you. Sometimes, these same people aren't receptive to your words of faith. What's a *faith-filled* person to do? Follow Naomi's lead: she spoke a blessing over Boaz even though he wasn't present. She trusted that God desired to bless Boaz, and she was acting in faith that He would. Faith pleases God.

Her mother-in-law then said to her; "Where did you glean today and where did you work? May he who took notice of you be blessed." And Naomi said to her daughter-in-law, "May he be blessed of the LORD who has not withdrawn his kindness to the living and to the dead." (Ruth 2:19,20 NASB)

Cal and I have acted upon this principle of releasing spoken blessings over people who cannot hear us. Sometimes, actual miles separate us, but, in other situations, the conditions of hearts and emotions have been the separating factor. You may have similar situations in your lives, too. Even though you live under the same roof, family members are often isolated from each other. God wants unity: a house divided falls. So, during our prayer time every morning, we have spoken blessings over loved ones.

May you, _____, love the Lord with all your heart, soul, mind and strength.

May you truly love your neighbor as yourself.

May others see in you the love of Christ.

May God stir within you all the gifts and callings He has planned and purposed for your life.

May you seek Him and understand His ways.

May you embrace His truth, so it becomes your rule of conduct.

May you walk in a manner worthy of His calling.

May God give you wisdom beyond your years, surpassing your training and knowledge.

May all that you do be done to honor Him.

In Jesus' Name, Amen.

[insert person's name], may the Lord be your shield and your defense.

May you be afraid of no one.

May He bring you comfort through His word, His worship and through His warfare.

May you be strong in the Lord and in the power of His might.

May you tear down the strongholds that bind and restrict your walking in His covenant promises.

May you know Him as your Victor.

In Jesus' Name, Amen.

We are God's ambassador proclaiming His truth and eternal destiny for His people. With great confidence, we can draw near to the throne of God, asking for and receiving His mercy and grace for ourselves and for others. (Hebrews 4:16) God will give us the words to speak to make known with boldness His word of truth. His truth dispels lies. Lies trap and hinder people from becoming all that God purposed for them, aborting their eternal inheritance.

We didn't give up.

---

5. Just as Jesus is *preparing a place for us* (John 14:2), prepare your heart and life for children *yet to be born* into your family, whether through your natural body, foster care or through adoption. Begin speaking aloud the fruitfulness of your body, male or female. Cal and I spoke blessings over our bodies and our union many years before David was conceived. We didn't give up. We had to walk by faith and not by sight. Our physical bodies were aging, but we chose to believe the report of the Lord that children are His blessing (Psalm 127:3-5). God desires to give good gifts to us. Such tenacity is often needed, even in the lives of other couples desiring children. Cal and I have spoken blessings of fruitfulness and multiplication over others. We have coupled this with continual prayer for them, calling forth children who will be raised for the glory of God and for the furtherance of His Kingdom.

6. Even if your children are young, begin to bless their future spouse. Call forth the preparation of your child and his/her spouse for a holy union, preserving their purity, righteousness and unity in the oneness of Christ. Cal and I began doing this many years ago. We continue to bless our children, their spouses and their children. Both Rebecca and Isaac brought individual blessings into their marriage which worked together to fulfill God's eternal destiny for them as a couple and for their descendants. Our eldest son, Anthony, and his precious wife, Cassidy, just celebrated their 20th anniversary. Anthony began praying for his future spouse when he was around 10. Cal and I joined his prayers with blessings for him and his future bride. Now, our blessings and prayers include their three wonderful sons: Andrew, Zachary and Daniel.

7. Exercise great faith in God as your provider as you speak blessings of success, prosperity and favor over your spouse. Identify their natural and supernatural abilities and encourage those areas with God's power-packed word. Undergird your spouse with blessings that build confidence in areas which challenge them. As Cal and I ride together to church on Sundays, I speak blessings over him as I massage his hands with cream. Rubbing his right hand, I speak:

May the Lord strengthen you as you serve others.

May your hands be anointed for the healing and comfort of others.

May the Lord reward your service.

May God prosper your work, causing you to gain wealth.

May you honor God from your wealth.

May you always be a cheerful giver.

May the Lord give you wisdom and counsel to do His work.

In Jesus' Name, Amen.

Then, I take his left hand, the one on which he wears our wedding band, and speak:

May our love for each other grow more perfect and complete.

May we be united in our love for the Lord and for each other.

May our love be sacrificial and full of joy.

The Spoken Blessing I: A Spiritual Posture

May the Lord bless our marriage with His presence.
May He use our marriage to bless others.
In Jesus' Name, Amen.

8. Allow your faith to be witnessed by other believers as you speak blessings over them. Every time you attend a church service, a class, a fellowship time or as you serve; ask God for and expect to encounter opportunities to bless. There is always someone in your path who needs God's blessing. Determine in your heart that you will be a blessing to the Body of Christ. You are God's ambassador. When you prepare your heart and focus your expectations, looking for blessing opportunities, your fellowship times will always be exciting and rewarding. Attending *church* will never be the same!

God's will is to bless.

---

9. Remember: out of nothing can come something. God has shown us that fact from the beginning. We know and have experienced the power of speaking and declaring God's living word. His life-depositing word continues to grow and produce good fruit within us. Begin to speak blessings with confidence in Him.

If you live in a rural community, speak blessings of productivity and prosperity over the land. If the small towns in your area appear to be *drying up,* speak God's life over them. Speak blessings over your sphere of influence. Deuteronomy 28:3 (NASB) proclaims: *"Blessed shall you be in the city, and blessed shall you be in the country."* God's will is to bless. Declare these blessings into your sphere of influence:

May these fields be fruitful and multiply.
May the earth become rich with nutrients and minerals.
May the seed planted take root and grow, producing a bountiful harvest.
May these crops be protected from destructive forces.
May the rains come at the proper time and in the needed amounts.
May the Lord give the farmers wisdom and instruction for the benefit of their investment.

May these farmers honor the Lord with their first fruits, returning to Him a tenth of all their earnings.

May they praise and bless His Name.

In Jesus' Name, Amen.

May the commerce of this town begin to flourish.

May life, not death, be restored to this area.

May a quickening occur within the minds and hearts of these businessmen and women, showing them how to operate in a profitable way.

May God's favor surround their businesses, drawing others to use their services and to buy their products.

May these owners operate their stores and lives in a manner worthy of the Lord.

May they honor Him in all their ways.

May the Lord cause their hands to prosper.

In Jesus' Name, Amen."

Your city, state and country will greatly benefit from your boldly proclaiming blessings over them. Read the Amplified Bible's version of Proverbs 11:11:

"By the blessing of the influence of the upright and God's favor [because of them] the city is exalted, but it is overthrown by the mouth of the wicked."

Your influence upon your homeland carries weight and value. Become informed and sensitive to the needs of your city, state and country. Listen to the events which are occurring and address those specific needs within your blessings. With great faith, declare them over your land. God will honor your faith and will accomplish His plan.

"For the eyes of the LORD are in every place, Watching the evil and the good." (Proverbs 15:3 NASB)

The Spoken Blessing I: A Spiritual Posture

"For the eyes of the LORD move to and fro throughout the earth that He may strongly support those whose heart is completely His..."
(II Chronicles 16:9 NASB)

{A Call to the Nation© blessing set was written for releasing blessings over our nation. Visit our website: www.spokenblessing.com to discover more about our Blessing sets.}

10. If you need time to develop your confidence in *speaking* blessings, try this:

a. Write a note, even a Thank You card, to someone and include a simple blessing.

"May the Lord bless you with His presence.
May He return to you the kindness you have shown me.
May He honor your compassionate heart.
In Jesus' Name, Amen."

b. Send an e-mail to a college-aged child, to a friend or a business associate and include a blessing. In your blessing, address something that is important to them, i.e.: high test scores, financial support, success in their career, wisdom for parenting, etc. When you speak about something that is important to them and call upon God for His help, they will take notice.

c. If your spouse travels, write a blessing on a 3 x 5 card and slip it into their overnight bag. God's word of truth and your love will encourage their day.

May God bless your going out and your coming in.
May His favor surround you like a shield.
May others honor the character of Christ they see in you.
May God give you wisdom in your business.
May His Spirit direct your thoughts.
May you respond to His leading.
May you always remember that God loves you with an everlasting love that doesn't end.
In Jesus' Name, Amen.

d. If your spouse is not receptive for such an overt expression of your faith, *go undercover,* literally. A friend placed blessings under her husband's side of their bed, between the mattress and box springs.

Once she began doing this, she testified to noticing a difference in his mental and spiritual attitudes. She coupled this effort with speaking blessings over him out of range of his hearing and continually prayed for him and his salvation. Remember, it is the power of God, present through His penetrating word, which accomplishes His work of redemption, restoration, healing, deliverance, etc. This same power was at work through Peter's shadow (Acts 5:15) and Paul's handkerchiefs and aprons (Acts 19:11-12). It is not the piece of paper or cloth, but the anointing: the powerful presence of God that operates through something or someone to perform His will. God's life-depositing word carries His anointing.

e. If your children are in the public school system, you can share God's blessings in several ways:

i. for his teachers, prepare baked goods or candy bags and attach a blessing to each bag,

ii. during Teacher Appreciation Week, place a written blessing in every teacher's "mailbox;"

iii. during Thanksgiving activities in which parents participate, share a written blessing and note of thanks for their faithful support. Keep in mind that every child is helped when parents give of their time and resources.

f. If your children attend a faith-based school, your efforts could include the children. A friend has shared blessings with her son's classmates year after year. She has found creative ways to distribute blessings to these students who look forward to receiving them. Some students have taken their blessing home and shared it with their parents! What precious treasures have been given by this one mother! You can do this as well.

The Spoken Blessing I: A Spiritual Posture

g. At a gathering of friends (i.e.: a ladies' luncheon, or a dinner for couples), place a blessing at the place setting of each guest. Ask each guest to read aloud their blessing. As each blessing is read, God's uplifting word is multiplied beyond just the individual reading it. The atmosphere of your gathering is transformed into one of honoring God and focusing on His work within the lives of your guests. As I have attended luncheons in which this was done, I have heard the guests testify that their blessing specifically addressed a need in their life. This has truly humbled me to witness the power of God and His loving-kindness.

h. During the early 1990's, I served as the children's pastor for Christian Heritage Church in Tallahassee, Florida. Desiring to develop a different approach to observing the Advent Season, the Lord gave me *a witty invention*: the Blessing Wreath. The first one developed had twenty-four written blessings attached to it. Each blessing was rolled and tied with ribbon. Also, special treats wrapped in colorful fabric were tied to the evergreen wreath. The wreath was placed on a table with a pillar candle positioned within its center. Beginning with the first Sunday in December, the candle was lit, and a child was invited to select a blessing from the wreath. I spoke that blessing over the child and the others in attendance, then, that child selected a special candy.

Within our Children's Church services throughout December, we discussed the anticipation of Jesus coming into our lives and doing great things in us and through us. We honored who Jesus is, God with us, as the blessings focused our attention on Him and His presence within our lives. Such a time of spiritual reflection encouraged *making room* for Jesus to live and operate within our hearts and homes.

Parents chose to incorporate these Blessing Wreaths within their families' Advent devotions.

On December 1st, the candle was lit at dinnertime and a child selected a blessing which was read aloud over him and others. The children chose a treat after the blessing was spoken. Each night a different child chose a blessing, yet all heard the spoken word for their life. The speaking of these blessings offered opportunities for family discussions about the meaning of the blessing and their expectations of God's doing great things in their lives.

Reading these prepared blessings allowed parents time to become familiar with the idea of speaking blessings. The pressure of preparing something to speak was removed. Over time, the parents observed the excitement of their children wanting their blessing read. As the evenings progressed, parents felt more comfortable with speaking blessings. To complete the thirty-one days of December, parents were encouraged to create and write blessings which were personalized for their children and their specific needs and interests. Something so very simple has been powerful and significant in the lives of children. They desperately need encouragement and affirmations. They need to hear of God's love for them and witness the faith of their parents.

My desire is for families to develop the practice of speaking blessings over each other. If you are interested in using the Advent Blessing Wreath in your family, business, Sunday School, church or school, visit: spokenblessing.com to learn more about *Cornerstone of God's Word*©. Begin a new tradition which honors the Lord and encourages excitement for life and hope for the future!

Learn to bless God. One of the reasons for speaking blessings over people is to turn their attention to God and to focus on His character and nature. We must do the same. As we experience His power and presence within our lives and recognize His blessings flowing into our lives, praise will pour from our hearts. We will honor Him with our lips. We will exalt Him with our worship. Psalms 145-150 are beautiful examples of blessing our God. Consider the various attributes of God's character that are identified: great, glorious, majestic, powerful, good, gracious, merciful, everlasting, righteous, just, delivering, protective, supportive, healing, providing, creative, etc. Declare these attributes and ascribe them to God. As we learn how to bless Him, we will be endued with His power. It never fails.

When I bless and thank Him for who He is, I declare His nature over my loved ones, myself and over every situation. Consequently, I am empowered with confidence in His presence operating within my life.

Try this. Focus on Him. With a pure heart, honor Him with your words. Declare who He is over your life. In blessing God, you will be blessed.

11. Speak blessings filled with life, restoration and peace over those struggling with health problems: body, soul or spirit. Jesus came to give us life and life abundantly. Recall His explanation and declaration as found in John 10:10 (TPT): *"A thief has only one thing in mind---he wants to steal, slaughter, and destroy. But I have come to give you everything in abundance, more than you expect—life in its fullness until you overflow!"*

You will encounter people with varying types and degrees of illnesses. Jesus is the Healer of all conditions and diseases. Even if the illness has caused a loss of mental acuteness, you can exercise faith and speak God's life-depositing word to the person's spirit. Jesus will honor your faith and respond to your declared blessings just as He did to the centurion's faith which is documented in Matthew 8:5-13. Every person has an eternal spirit which does not *shut down*, even if the mind does. Declaring God's life-depositing word, speak spirit to spirit.

12. Catch the Lord's vision of your being His ambassador. As you declare His spoken word into people's lives, you are expressing and imparting the King's will into their lives. When you accept the ministry of reconciliation and begin to use the word of reconciliation, you become a vital link to the eternal restoration of thousands. Restoring people to their *right relationship* with the Father is the reason for Jesus' humbling Himself to become a human, suffering death on the cross and receiving His new resurrected life. You honor and exalt Jesus' life, death and resurrection when you speak blessings over others.

My Blessing for You

May you be kind and tender-hearted to others, forgiving them, just as God in Christ has forgiven you.

May you bless others, even when they curse or mistreat you.

May God sow His life-changing seed into your life.

May you become a tree firmly planted by streams of water, which yields its fruit in its season, and whose leaf does not wither.

May you sow the seeds of life and truth.

May you reap a great harvest of righteousness.

May God cause you to prosper in whatever you do.

May whatever you do be done to the glory of God.

In Jesus' Name, Amen.

The Spoken Blessing I: A Spiritual Posture

Journal of My Journey with the Spoken Blessing

Refer to Luke 7:11-17, in which Jesus redirected the widow's focus from her dead son to glorifying God for His marvelous, miraculous deed. Examine your outlook on life. List areas that need a new approach. Explain what you will do to change your heart, your focus and your confession to one of life, hope and confidence in the Lord.

_____
_____
_____
_____

How do you plan to keep your heart and your speech pure?

_____
_____
_____
_____

What scriptures have made the most impact on confirming to you the necessity, validity, and power of speaking blessings over yourself and others, over your community and nation?

_____
_____
_____
_____

Interning with the Spoken Blessing

Write a blessing that will impart God's favor, blessing and increase into a person's life. Ask God for an opportunity to speak it over someone.

_____
_____
_____
_____

Do nothing from selfishness or empty conceit, but with humility of mind let each of you regard one another as more important than himself; do not merely look out for your own personal interests, but also for the interests of others." (Philippians 2:3-4 NASB)

Appendix

Examples of Blessings

1. Husbands, friends, co-workers, children:

"May the LORD reward your work, and your wages be full from the Lord, the God of Israel, under whose wings you have sought refuge." (Ruth 2:12)

"May God's favor surround you like a shield." (Psalm 5:12)

"May God cause you to prosper and excel in all that you do. May whatever you do bring honor and glory to God."
(Genesis 39:3; Colossians 3:17; I Peter 4:11)

2. Children:

"May the Lord protect you from all evil. May He keep your soul. May the Lord guard your going out and your coming in from this time forth and forever more." (Psalm 121:5-8)

This blessing can be used with different ages. Young children may become fearful of the dark, storms or scary noises. Older children may have concerns about attending a large high school, gangs, drugs, etc. Young adult children may feel uncertain about leaving for college.

"May you remember that you can do all things through Christ who strengthens you." (Philippians 4:13)

A child or teenager may struggle with a poor self-image. Remind them of the power of Jesus working within them through His Spirit. Read Psalm 139:14-18 to your child. Then declare this blessing over them:

"May God hold you in His loving arms, embracing you with His compassion. May you feel the warmth of His presence and know that He will never leave you or forsake you. You are His and He is yours." (Joshua 1:5)

This blessing can be applied to various situations of children being apart from their parents, i.e.: spending the night with a friend, attending summer camp, children leaving for college or beginning a new job.

"May you know that God has loved you with an everlasting love, and that He draws you to Him with His loving-kindness." (Jeremiah 31:3)

You could encourage and bless a child or friend who struggles with recognizing God's love for them. Some children have been told that they were *accidents* or a *mistake*. They need God's truth spoken to them. Some marriage relationships undermine the worth of a person. Help a friend know the value God places on them.

3. Friends:

"May the Lord be your Good Shepherd caring and providing for all your needs.

May He cause you to lie down in green pastures.

May He lead you beside quiet waters.

May He restore your soul." (Psalm 23:1-3)

Declare these encouraging words to a friend who is experiencing difficult circumstances.

Creating Blessings Based on God's Word

Use these scriptures to write blessings. Then, ask God for opportunities to declare them.

The LORD is your keeper; The LORD is your shade on your right hand.

The sun will not smite you by day, Nor the moon by night.

The LORD will protect you from all evil; He will keep your soul.

The LORD will guard your going out and your coming in From this time forth and forever. (Psalm 121:5-8 NASB)

May the Lord...

_____

_____

_____

_____

"For I know the plans I have for you,' declares the LORD, 'plans for welfare and not for calamity to give you a future and a hope.'"
(Jeremiah 29:11 NASB)

"and hope does not disappoint, because the love of God has been poured out within our hearts through the Holy Spirit who was given to us."
(Romans 5:5 NASB)

May you always remember...

_____

_____

_____

_____

"I will instruct you and teach you in the way which you should go;
I will counsel you with My eye upon you." (Psalm 32:8 NASB)

> *But let all who take refuge in you rejoice; let them ever sing for joy, and spread your protection over them, that those who love your name may exult in you. For you bless the righteous, O LORD; you cover him with favor as with a shield.* (Psalm 5:11,12 ESV)

May God instruct...

_____

_____

_____

_____

"That according to the riches of his glory he may grant you to be strengthened with power through his Spirit in your inner being, " (Ephesians 3:16 ESV)

"For God hath not given us the spirit of fear; but of power, and of love, and of a sound mind." (II Timothy 1:7 KJV)

May God strengthen you...

_____

_____

_____

_____

"For I am confident of this very thing, that He who began a good work in you will perfect it until the day of Christ Jesus." (Philippians 1:6 NASB)

"Be diligent to present yourself approved to God as a workman who does not need to be ashamed, handling accurately the work of truth"
(II Timothy 2:15 NASB)

May you be confident...

_____

_____

_____

_____

"Children, obey your parents in the Lord, for this is right. Honor your father and mother (which is the first commandment with a promise), that it may be well with you, and that you may live long on the earth."
Ephesians 6:1-3 NASB

May you obey...

_____

_____

_____

_____

Journal of My Journey with the Spoken Blessing

After speaking and declaring blessings over others, describe who you spoke to and how they responded.

_____
_____
_____
_____

Keep a journal of the blessings you create from the Scriptures and with whom you share them. Make observations of how the Lord responds to these blessings.

_____
_____
_____
_____

Note any unexpected responses to your spoken blessings. Describe your reactions to these responses.

_____
_____
_____
_____

"... while we have opportunity, let us do good to all men."
Galatians 6:10 NASB

Author's Note

I am grateful for your willingness to spend time with me. Time is a gift from God. I trust that your time was well spent---discovering the impact of God's word being spoken and declared over yourself and others. Did your relationship with Him deepen and become more special?

As you have read our family's story, you discovered that the biblically based principle was presented to us when our lives were a mess. With a heart filled with love and tenderness, our heavenly Father sent a truly humble servant-leader, Pastor Bill Ligon, to teach us and to turn our hearts back to the Him. Pastor Ligon's message of truth served as a lifeline back to the Father through His Son, Jesus, who is the Living Word.

Pastor Ligon sowed seeds of truth which took root, grew and bore fruit. You have tasted the fruit from those seeds. I trust that you have been nourished and strengthened in your intimate walk with the Father. May you continually enjoy and value all the benefits of the Salvation of Jesus. May you remain is close life-union with Him through the presence and empowerment of His Holy Spirit.

May you sow seeds of God's word upon the soil of men, women and children's hearts. May His Seed take root and thrive. May God receive the glory and honor from your faithful service.

Ann Dews Gleaton

About the Author:

Ann Dews Gleaton and family were introduced to the principle and the practice of speaking Blessings in 1991. Their family needed a major attitude adjustment! Learning to speak Blessings met this urgent need. Ann and her husband, Cal, followed the example of Jesus in declaring Blessings over their children. The attitude of their hearts and the atmosphere of their home changed.

Ann's passion is to teach men, women and children how to make The Spoken Blessing an integral part of their lives. She has multiplied this understanding and practice within numerous lives. Ann has taught within various settings: college courses, women's conferences, and Bible studies for men and women. She and Cal minister to others the life-changing words of Christ as they follow His example of speaking and releasing Blessings.

Ann and Cal currently live in Cairo, Georgia. Their four children, now married, deposit God's word into their children's lives. The principle and practice of speaking Blessings is propelled into the next generation, for the glory of God.

To order the sequel to this book: *The Spoken Blessing---Influencing Generations* and to learn more about available Blessing sets, please visit: *www.spokenblessing.com*

The Gleaton Family

Cal and Ann Gleaton

Kyle and Elizabeth Del Vecchio
Joseph, Isaac, Victoria, Noah and
Daniel (Left to Right)

Peyton and Amy Gleaton
Charlie, Rhett, Ruby and Reed
(Left to Right)

Anthony and Cassidy Gleaton
Andrew, Daniel and Zachary
(Left to Right)

David and Carolina Gleaton

References

Bowers, Freeda. *Give Me 40 Days*, Bridge-Logos Publishers, 2002.

Conner, Kevin. *Interpreting the Symbols and Types, Completed Revised and Expanded.* Portland: BT Publishing, 1980.

Gleaton, Ann D. *A Call to the Nation,* 1999.

Gleaton, Ann D. *Cornerstone of God's Word,* 1999.

Gleaton, Ann D. *Hope, the Anchor of the Soul,* 2004.

Harley, Jr., Willard F. *His Needs Her Needs*, Fleming H. Revell, 2001.

Ligon, Sr., William T. *Imparting the Blessing to Your Children*, Shalom, Inc., 1989.

Lockyer, Dr. William, R.S.L. *All the Women of the Bible, All the Divine Names & Titles in the Bible,* Zondervan Publishing House, 1975.

McGee, Robert S. *Father Hunger*, Servant Publications, 1993.

Meyers, Rick. *e-Sword X the Sword of the LORD with an electronic edge,* (9.5 version), 2025.

Pierce, Chuck D. *Seven Days of Stillness: A Prayer Focus to Renew Your Spirit*, 08-31-04, Glory of Zion International Ministries.

Ryrie, Charles, C., Th.D., Ph.D. *The Ryrie Study Bible*, New American Standard Translation, Moody Press, 1978.

Sevrens, Julie. *Tallahassee Democrat*, "Forgiveness can heal," 08-02-99, Knight Ridder.

Simmons, Brian. *The Passion Translation,* BroadStreet Publishing Group, 2020.

Stamps, D. and Adams, J. (Eds.) (2011) *Fire Bible: English Standard Version,* Hendrickson Publishers Marketing, LLC.

Strong, James, LL.D., S.T.D. *The New Strong's Exhaustive Concordance of the Bible*, Thomas Nelson Publishers, 1990.

The Lockman Foundation. *The Amplified Bible*, Zondervan, 1987.

Vine, W.E. *Vine's Expository Dictionary of Old and New Testament Words*, Marshall, Morgan & Scott, Publications, Ltd., 1981.

Webster's New World Dictionary of the American Language, The World Publishing Company, 1968.

Whiston, William, A.M. *The Works of Josephus*, Hendrickson Publishers, 1987.

Wilkinson, Bruce with David Kopp. *A Life God Rewards*, Multnomah Publishers, Inc., 2002.

Zodhiates, Spiros, Th.D. *The Hebrew-Greek Key Study Bible*, King James Version, Baker Book House, 1984.

www.ingramcontent.com/pod-product-compliance
Lightning Source LLC
Chambersburg PA
CBHW060656100426
42734CB00047B/1951